SHARE AND GROW *Rich*

MICHAEL MACFARLANE
with Warren Jamison

Published by Elevate, Charleston, South Carolina.
Member of Advantage Media Group.

ELEVATE is a registered trademark and the
Elevate colophon is a trademark of Advantage Media Group, Inc.

Printed in the United States of America.

ISBN: 978-1-60194-008-7

Most Advantage Media Group titles are available at special quantity discounts for bulk purchases for sales promotions, premiums, fundraising, and educational use. Special versions or book excerpts can also be created to fit specific needs.

For more information, please write: Special Markets, Advantage Media Group, P.O. Box 272, Charleston, SC 29402 or call 1.866.775.1696.

Library of Congress Cataloging-in-Publication Data

MacFarlane, Michael, 1969-
Share and grow rich : the Dottie Walters effect / by Michael MacFarlane with Warren Jamison.
p. cm.
Includes bibliographical references and index.
ISBN 978-1-60194-008-7 (alk. paper)
1. Walters, Dottie. 2. Success in business. 3. Marketing. 4. Selling. 5. Success.
I. Jamison, Warren. II. Title.
HF5386.M183 2007
658.85--dc22

2007042816

SHARE AND GROW Rich

The Dottie Walters Effect

How Her Secret of Generosity Launched So Many Stellar Careers, and What It Can Do for Yours

MICHAEL MACFARLANE
with Warren Jamison

Table of Contents

Now is the only time there is.
Make your now wow, your minutes miracles,
and your days pay.

——MARK VICTOR HANSEN

An investment in knowledge pays the best interest.

——BENJAMIN FRANKLIN

1

The Dottie Walters Effect— What Worked Great for Her Will Work Great for You

· THE SECRET OF SUCCESS: SHARE · GIVING AWAY TOO MUCH · HOW TO CREATE SHARING VALUE · DOTTIE'S SOLUTION · THE DOTTIE WALTERS EFFECT ·

In later chapters, we'll show you what many people wrote about the powerful effect Dottie had on them. But first let's talk about what you can gain from knowing about her actions and methods. They can revolutionize your life in ways you want to have happen, just as they did for hundreds of thousands of people during her lifetime, and will continue to do for millions more. Her influence lives on in the memories of those whose lives she touched and in her books.

The Secret of Success: Share

In the beginning, Dottie's first sharings were mostly benefits she received: the gift of a ream of paper, a typewriter borrowed, an exchange of babysitting time and other ordinary things. They were all vital at that fragile stage of her career. Although the extremely fragile phase — her first steps into business — ended in a few weeks, those early days of struggle had an enormous, and permanent, impact on her. She began a lifelong habit of sharing her ever growing knowledge about advertising, selling, and a host of other topics. By all appearances, this habit came naturally to her; just as clear is the fact that she built on her early success with the concept of sharing.

So when she first heard the saying, *"Give a man a fish and you may feed him for a day, teach him how to fish and you feed him for a lifetime,"* she knew exactly what the old sage meant. If you give or lend someone something of value, money for example, you must diminish your own reserves in order to increase the recipient's resources. But if you share your expertise with someone, you still have all your expertise. Knowledge is endlessly reproducible without affecting your possession of it.

Giving Away Too Much

But if you share — that is, give your expertise away — is anything left that people will pay to hear or read?

If that can happen — if your expertise is so limited that people can acquire all of it in a phone call or by reading an email — the problem is obvious: you simply don't have enough of it. This means your most pressing task is to deepen, broaden and refine your expertise in your particular niche.

Consider how this is working in computer software. Throughout the 1990s, a massive movement of tectonic power was developing a virtually virus-proof and hacker-proof operating system called Linux — to be given away. By 2000, it was complete with word processing, email, a browser called Mozilla Firefox, and Gnucash for keeping track of bank accounts.

Growing numbers of corporations and institutions are switching, or considering switching, to Linux. IBM, Google, Amazon, and eBay have already done so. The reasons? The software works better, costs less and lasts longer.

However, no single company controls Linux, which is not a software company in the sense that Microsoft is. Nevertheless, a huge amount of open source software is already available.

Customizing Linux to each corporation's special needs calls for specialized knowledge. Enter companies such as OpenSourcery.com of Portland Oregon. This company, and others like it, know what's best in open source software, where to find it, how to customize it to individual needs, how to make the installation, and how to train people in its use.

Many people feel they must guard their knowledge carefully so that they can sell it. This is the scarcity concept — restrict your expertise so you can sell it for more money, which generally means you sell less to fewer people.

But do you ever share *all* your expertise? Could you do that even if you tried? When you share as much as you can for free, you whet an audience's appetite for more. Thus sharing becomes the most powerful selling tool ever conceived for expertise.

How to Create Sharing Value

How do you acquire valuable information to share? By studying and refining what you know in your knowledge niche so you can present it to other people in easily understood terms. As Dottie would say, quoting Albert Einstein, "The solution is at hand." You already know much if not most of what you need to know to be an expert in your field. Here are the three most important keys to making *sharing value creation* effective: simplify, amplify, glorify.

If you are a public speaker, you routinely polish your knowledge and refine it for presentation to audiences. It only takes a slightly different approach to make that knowledge suitable for sharing in one-on-one situations — as, for example, when you're on the phone with someone who wants you to mentor them. What is that person? He or she is an ideal candidate to attend one of your workshops, where you spend a weekend delivering the full load of your expertise a group of people for fees that total an amount that interests you.

Creating valuable knowledge you can share is a simple, four-step procedure that always works — if you make it work

1. Alert your subconscious mind that you want to develop useful knowledge that you can share with other people. It's easy unless you're convinced that any kind of mental effort is a hard and painful thing. All you have to do is think of what you want to create.

(How do you *alert your subconscious mind?*

You think intensely about what you want to achieve. As you do this, think about the successes you're pursuing and how you'll enjoy having achieved them. Visualize the results you seek in the most vivid terms you can imagine.

When your subconscious mind is fully alert to what you want to achieve in the way of adding to your expertise, supporting ideas will start popping into your head and you'll find yourself noticing helpful items as you read news magazines or watch the nightly news.)

2. Write out your statement of intention (SI). Keep your SI simple and direct. Revise and update the latest version of your SI every day, or at least frequently, until you're well on your way to developing the knowledge you'll share. By putting your subconscious on the prowl for shareable knowledge in this way, you will start finding useful bits and pieces — your building blocks of shareable knowledge — in almost everything you read. Your reading will often provide leads to big chunks of useful information. In this way you'll be doing what Dottie did: recombining old knowledge gleaned from books and other sources into something fresh and to herself. You can do the same. You can create something fresh and unique by blending old knowledge gleaned from books and other sources with your special take on life.

3. Commit your knowledge-offering to the world on paper or a computer screen. Study it. Revise and refine it. Read it aloud into a recorder. Play it back so you can spot passages needing refinement.

4. Share your knowledge with others at every appropriate opportunity to increase the market for your seminars and speaking events. If possible, devise some means of acquiring email addresses with permission to send invitations to your events and news about your activities.

Dottie's Solution

When she shared her marvelous insights and ideas for becoming a more successful speaker, several outstanding aspects of Dottie's personality were evident. She shared information with an empathetic and genuine interest in meeting the other person's needs. She didn't think about whether the other person might become a valuable customer; she didn't rank them as to their importance in achieving her own goals; she treated everyone with the same warmth and encouraging manner regardless of their circumstances. Rich or poor, beginner or veteran all were treated alike. Her desire was simply to help other people accomplish what they wanted to do. This focus on other people's goals enabled her to concentrate on them, on their needs and potentialities. In other words, she forgot about herself when working with other people.

And Dottie appeared to do this effortlessly — a state she reached only after working hard with that result in mind. How did she achieve this incomparable ability? She studied the field of public speaking intensely. She refined, adapted and polished bits of knowledge that many speakers did not have — particularly newbies or those standing on the sidelines thinking about starting a career as a public speaker. She put energy and time into paring her material down to small but helpful bits that she could deliver in a few seconds.

This approach was powered by Dottie's sincerity in wanting to help the other person any way she could. Genuine sincerity is unmistakable; it can't be faked. But it can be learned and made into a potent wealth-building skill by people willing to work at fostering it in themselves. Probably the most effective tool for bringing this about are self-composed affirmations that describe exactly how you will put the other person's needs ahead of your own.

Dottie perfected a quick way to capture a person's attention and to make a powerful impact on them in the brief encounters that occur whenever people gather at networking opportunities such as Chamber of Commerce meetings or trade shows. Dottie soon realized that handing out business cards — and collecting batches of them in return — accomplishes little.

We don't know how long it took Dottie to solve this problem, but my guess is that she did it fast, maybe instantaneously. Her solution was simple and effective. Dottie's sincerity was always evident; her approach never sounded canned, her genuine interest in helping the other person meant her words were always fresh and well suited to the circumstances.

Yet, in spite of its obviousness, regardless of its power; few of us rise to the level where we regularly use Dottie's solution.

Why? Because the hard wiring in our heads makes us a thousand times more focused on ourselves and what we do than we are on someone else's achievements, goals and hopes and how we can help them. Self-centeredness is an outgrowth of every creature's fixation on its, his or her survival; this means it takes focused determination to overcome this natural bias in favor of our personal concerns, dreams and desires.

Yet, as Dottie's life and accomplishments prove, the most powerful way to make an impression on another person is to be interested in what they're doing. Not as a ploy to gain their attention so you can deliver your whole spiel, but because you genuinely want to connect with each person. As people who met Dottie discovered, she was genuinely interested in their challenges, ever ready to offer encouragement and helpful advice. As a result, she had a powerful effect on anyone who spent more than a few seconds in her presence.

Was this wholly altruistic on her part? No, and that's the beauty of her approach. Dottie knew that by sharing her knowledge as widely as she could, she expanded her influence, and that of her organization. The rewards would come and she understood how to make that happen as well.

The Dottie Walters Effect

From Jack Nichols:

> While rereading some of the e-mails that flew between me and Dottie and from some of the people I had referred to Dottie, the one below stood out — not because it was real special, but because it was not the least bit special. It summed up countless other messages that expressed much the same emotions. It epitomized what the Dottie effect was — and continues to be in the hearts and minds of all who knew her, had been in the audience at one of her events or read her books.
>
> Dottie was a speaker at one of our events in Toastmasters International and she offered to coach anyone in the room for half an hour for free. Carolyn and Soraya were both there along with about 75 other people. This was a follow-up to that offer. After the coaching session, Carolyn sent Dottie this e-mail that Dottie forwarded to me.

It was so much the norm with Dottie that it was expected. Yet how often do we get far more than we pay for? How often do we get loved, educated, motivated and challenged in an hour or less that will change the course of our lives? That was the Dottie effect. Over the years I have sent many people to hear Dottie and never did one say the time and money was not very well spent. I consider it a special privilege to have known Dottie as close as I did for so many years. However, it was even more special because I was able to help so many blooming speakers move along that professional speaker's path by taking them to see Dottie.

——Jack Nichols

Carolyn Cousins-Goldman to Dottie via email, copy to Jack Nichols:

Hello Jack, I want to share this email to Dottie with you:

Dear Dottie and Deborah,

Thank you so much for yesterday. Soraya, my husband and myself enjoyed meeting both of you. Deborah, you were more than helpful on the phone and yesterday Dottie, you spent so much more time than the 1/2 hour consultation. Thank you so much. We all learned so much from you, and we appreciate that no end.

I certainly am more on my way towards my goals since I now have a goal, thanks to your words of advice!

We all appreciated not only your time, Dottie, but your welcoming us into your home and your life, and showing us your family pictures, as well as your loves (your husband and Benjamin Franklin). Your office and your home was so unexpected and such a treat!

I can certainly see why you are so successful and such a wonderful speaker, Dottie. You make everyone around you feel so special! That's a rare and priceless gift;

I learned such a major lesson from you yesterday, you have no idea!

—Carolyn Goldman

From Allan Wallace:

> Dottie often talked about one of her Scottish grandparents, "My grandfather and his younger brother were orphans who came to America in a sailing ship. He told me, 'Remember, Lassie, we Scots may get knocked down, but we *never stay down!*'
>
> "He was a great inventor — we have his patents. I asked him one time when I was just a little girl, 'Grandpa, what is an engineer?' He replied, 'An engineer *drives the dream*.' " Dottie went on, "You are the engineer, the only engineer your dreams will ever have."
>
> Asked which saying had affected her most deeply, Dottie said, "One of the greatest quotations I ever read was from Amelia Earhart, the great American pilot. Earhart wrote:
>
> 'Some of us have great runways — already built for us.
>
> If you have one —TAKE OFF!
>
> But if you do not have one, then UNDERSTAND —
>
> It is your OWN RESPONSIBILITY TO GRAB A SHOVEL!
>
> And to BUILD ONE FOR YOURSELF —
>
> And for ALL THOSE WHO WILL SURELY FOLLOW YOU.'

Dottie not only built many runways, she also provided shovels to those of us that were working on other runways.

——Allan Wallace, Rector, Bastiat Free University.

Action is the real measure of intelligence.

—NAPOLEON HILL

2

Selling Power Comes from Developing Your Own Personal Selling Style

· The Practical Rationale for Sharing · How to Work a Room Effectively · Dottie's Big Secret—Hidden in Plain View All the Time · Dottie's Signature Story · Dottie's Sales Technique · Develop Your Own Sales System · The Tenuous but often Tight Connection between Giveaways and Higher Fees · The Formula You've Got to Beat · Dottie Walters Helping Hands Award ·

These pages are filled with accolades for how Dottie Walters lived, worked, made countless sales and became a legendary figure in many fields. Much of her celebrity comes from the fact that she, like Lindbergh, did it first. She was the first to write a book for saleswomen. She was first with a Hospitality Hostess Service in many cities, and then as the founder or co-founder of several of today's thriving organizations.

This is to say that no one else can sell themselves and their knowledge, expertise, products and services in exactly the same way Dottie did — for the simple reason that time has marched on. While no one can fully emulate her, everyone can learn from the principles she followed, which apply as well today as they did when she started.

Much well-deserved and heartfelt praise and admiration — from a few of the many people who benefited from Dottie's eagerness to share her expertise — is featured in later chapters. Many who basked in the warmth of her power-building encouragement have gone on to achieve great personal success. In her professional roles, Dottie unfailingly displayed that wonderful ability. Did her devotion to sharing spring from innate selfless goodness or from an instinctive knowledge that sharing would be highly profitable?

We'll never be certain of the answer. We do know that she encouraged everyone she met at professional gatherings — often with life-changing results. And we know that her businesses were highly successful, money-making enterprises.

The Practical Rationale for Sharing

Early in her career Dottie realized what sharing could do. It would enhance her reputation, widen her influence, bring her more friends and opportunities for further personal growth, and build her company and its profits more rapidly than any other method could. All those things would enable her to obtain higher fees and prices for what she did and boost sales of her books and other products.

The point of this book is that sharing expertise and encouraging others is one of the most powerful profit builders known to humankind. Let's examine a specific situation that all of us are likely to encounter: the networking event. That means any meeting where many people are there to make new business contacts, say a Chamber of Commerce meeting.

The most common — and least effective — way of operating at such a meeting is to walk in with a pocket full of your business cards and try to pass out as many as possible.

You have within your own experience the reason why this procedure doesn't accomplish much. You get home after the meeting with a pocket full of cards, but now they are not all yours, now they include the business cards you collected from people you exchanged cards with. Well and good so far, but what did you do with the cards you collected?

At best, you'll skim through them, pick out a few that you intend to write to or phone — but probably won't because you can't remember anything about the person. The rest you toss in a drawer where they'll lay for months until you eventually trash them. But you have planted *your* cards with lots of people, right? Surely you'll hear from at least a few of them. But you don't because your cards went in the trash all over town just like the ones you collected did.

What's the alternative? Our heroine shows us the way:

How to Work a Room Effectively

Dottie didn't go into meetings intent on telling everybody who'd listen about the great books she'd written and the wonderful magazine she published. She asked people what they did and she was genuinely interested in their plans and purposes. She would ask for their cards and often jot a note on the back. And, within a few days, she would call to discuss what they were doing and how she could help them do it better.

"Well, sure," you can think. "That worked for Dottie because she published a magazine, was a consummate public speaker, and had enormous contacts — but will it work for me?"

Why not?

Dottie wasn't born with any of those assets: she created them. Dottie was able to do that because she always focused on the other person's needs and how she could help them. Sometimes she benefited financially, more often she didn't. But she always made a connection, a lasting impression. She worked tirelessly at creating a buzz about her activities so that people would urge their friends to get in touch with her. Her most effective means were indirect. She was a master of guerilla marketing many years before that term became a buzz word. Here's how she did it.

At many events where business and professional people gather, you're likely to encounter a real estate agent or an insurance salesperson. Let's assume that people in those occupations are not prospects for what you do. Should you break off your conversation as quickly as you can and continue your search for someone who is a more likely prospect?

Bad idea. Let's look at what you are really there for — even if you haven't thought of it in these terms. You're there to connect with as many people as possible. A connection means the other person will remember you and may refer prospective clients. This is fundamentally different from a contact. When your intention is to simply speak to a lot of people, exchange business cards and promises to call each other, what usually happens? You and all your new contacts forget each other in the blur of meeting many new people.

What is the net result of spending time making *contacts*? Usually nothing. It's generally a waste of time. You might as well have stayed home and watched professional athletes bang a ball or each other around on TV.

But what is the net result of making several *connections* at that same gathering? You will have made a memorable impression on — a connection with — let's say, eight people. Over the next week or so, you call all eight of them and pursue your discussions of what they're doing and how you can help. What does this make them do? It *compels* them to ask what your interests are.

Dottie's Big Secret – Hidden in Plain View All the Time

Here's the idea to plant in their minds. If the person you're speaking to sells something: real estate, insurance, software, industrial pumps, dental services — whatever — ask them, "Who would be an ideal prospect for you?"

Jot their answer on the back of their business card. Among the three hundred people you know, one or several are likely to be a good fit for each of your new connections. Connect each of those pairs in an appropriate way and you will have made a life-long friend of your new connection and usually will solidify your old relationship.

Most of your connections will feel driven to reciprocate in some way. This was Dottie's secret: never asking *for* anything, simply helping any way she could and relying on human nature to work its will on some of the people some of the time.

What made her approach so heart-warming and effective was that Dottie sincerely wanted to help the other person. The more genuine your dedication to helping others, the more Dottie's powerful system will help you. This is long-term strategy. You can pursue it vigorously while also hammering away with short term methods and strategies in pursuit of your short-term goals.

Dottie changed careers several times, and many of her connections held fast in her next career. For example, many of the merchants who bought ads in her Window Shopping column became the customers who launched her Hospitality Hostess Service. When Dottie began speaking at service clubs to speed the growth of her new hospitality business, she started in her local area where she already had many friends and connections.

Dottie's Signature Story

Dottie told this story to countless audiences. She would describe how she, as a young mother, was desperately trying to help her husband save their home from foreclosure. She pushed a stroller with her two babies over unpaved streets to the office of a local newspaper. Undeterred by a "No Help Wanted" sign in the newspaper's window, she talked the owner into giving her a wholesale rate on space in his paper — on credit.

Perhaps it was the most important sale of her life for three reasons: what she earned selling space to local merchants saved their home; it gave her the resources and confidence to launch a business a short time later that swiftly grew to several hundred employees, and it launched her on a lifetime of speaking and selling in her unique style.

It's a grand story, all the better because it's true. Dottie used it as an opener throughout her multiple careers to great effect. Her basic point could be stated in less colorful terms: that she was already behind when her race for success began. Dottie's purpose in telling her signature story, as she did, was to make the point that many people — perhaps *most* people — feel disadvantaged in some way. They don't have the education, or they feel that their physical deficiencies are held against them. Others believe — often with strong reason — that other factors beyond their control are holding them back. She sometimes made the point that such things do not in themselves hold people back; what does it is *their attitude toward those circumstances*. In other words, the real barrier to digging in to achieve more isn't whatever the problem might be; the real barriers are the limitations people place on themselves in their own minds. No matter what problem anyone has, dozens or even thousands of other people with the same difficulty have surmounted it. The barriers to success are established in your own mind, not in anyone else's mind.

Dottie's audiences were primarily well-educated members of the middle class. However, most of her events included people who seemed to believe — often with good cause — that their opportunities are limited in some way. Some are immigrants, who will be held back by their poor command of the English language until they make the effort to learn and, if necessary, take special training to eliminate an accent. It can be done if the will to do it is there.

However, none of that mattered to Dottie. She saw potential in everyone. She knew that most people can do enormously more than they believe they can; that what they need most is the self-confidence to do what they already know they must do to succeed.

Dottie's Sales Technique

So soft was Dottie's sales technique that most people didn't realize they had been persuaded to do something, perhaps buy something, more likely to persevere in their own quests for success and fulfillment.

Dottie's secret was to concentrate on the other person's needs and dreams. In the typical sales situation, she found getting involved in the other person's life and hopes would eventually compel reciprocation. It didn't always work right away. With some people it never worked at all. Far more often it worked beautifully — sometimes in wonderful and unexpected ways.

Develop Your Own Sales System

You may think of yourself as a public speaker, writer, researcher...whatever. The reality is that the most important — and to many, the most distasteful — part of your occupation is to sell yourself, your products, services and expertise. If this is a turnoff, get over it. Selling is as necessary and natural as breathing and, for most of us living in this culture, just as essential.

Selling is most efficiently done systematically. That is, by following specific steps. Let's take them from the top:

Step 1 — Obtain leads. A lead consists of the contact information that will *lead* you to a suspect: someone who may buy what you sell because he/she uses, needs or wants it.

Right here is where many reluctant sellers get stuck. They don't realize that more leads than they can handle are theirs if they systematically harvest them.

Here, but not listed in order of importance, are four ways to harvest a crop of leads:

> **A. Buy them.** This works for some occupations, but not at all for others. Several companies offer inexpensive leads. Research the Internet. As a general rule, you'll need to contact ten leads to find one who can be called a suspect.
>
> **B. Use printed directories.** Many of the best print directories can be found in the reference section of any good public library.
>
> **C. Research the Web.** Directories are easily found on the Internet. They usually have the latest information. Some are free, others are available on

yearly subscription. Public speakers should search for Event Planners and Meeting Directories using any combination of those words.

The Internet is an information organism that changes by the minute. What you can find today may not have existed yesterday and may be gone tomorrow. When you find something of considerable interest, copy it onto your own hard drive immediately. It could be the only time you'll ever see it.

D. Attend conferences, seminars, workshops and all the meetings you can. Work these rooms as suggested above under the heading *How to Work a Room Effectively*. Leads obtained this way are usually the best.

Step 2 — Contact your leads

Your object now is to convert leads into suspects. Choose among three options:

A. Phone them. Calls from strangers are widely seen as being more acceptable than spam. They're still intrusive. Keep this in mind and be very polite. After a rude reaction, immediately call your next lead. Keep going until you get a positive response.

B. Email them. If you already have some connection, emphasize it in your message. Do everything you can to avoid sending spam messages, or some that look like spam. Otherwise you're likely to get nasty, flaming replies.

C. Snail mail them. Design your mailing so it doesn't look like mass-produced junk mail, 60 to 90 percent of which gets dumped in the trash without being opened. Few people object to receiving a personalized, individually written letter with a stamp on its envelope. Not only is snail mail the least intrusive, for many people it's uncommon — so they pay more attention.

In most sales situations, your purpose in contacting leads is not to sell them. It's to arrange an appointment for a face-to-face meeting, a phone call at a mutually convenient time, or to get their permission to send them your demo tape, press kit, or whatever you send to prospective buyers. In the latter case, mention that you'll make a follow-up call and set a convenient time to do so if you can.

Step 3 — Sell your prospects

Create a benefits script that describes all the benefits your products or service will bring them. This means writing what you plan to say so that you can polish the words until you present a lot of points in vivid language. Use common words, and avoid jargon or slang that your prospect may not understand; they'll be annoyed rather than impressed.

Eliminate passive sentences; choose active verbs instead. When you deliver your benefits script in person or on the phone, speak clearly and not too fast. Your benefits script will present a lot of ideas that are unfamiliar to your prospects, so don't leave them behind. Also have a second and third version of your benefits script so you can repeat the benefits — but not with the exact same words.

Avoid sounding like you're delivering a canned pitch. You are, of course, but it's enormously more effective if it's not obvious. This means you have to practice until you always deliver your script with enthusiastic clarity. Mumbling, slurring words. talking fast or in a bored tone all tell the other party that you're delivering a canned pitch. What is their impression? That you aren't sincere; you don't care about them; you only want to make the sale. All that is the opposite of the Dottie Walters' sales philosophy and method.

Know your benefits script so well that you can smoothly omit parts that don't apply to the prospect you're talking to.

Step 4 — Seek prospect comment

After you have given your benefits script, close your mouth. Look at them expectantly and say nothing until they speak. Your silence will force them to say something. They may ask for additional information but more likely, they will come up with an objection.

Step 5 — Be prepared for objections

You must be ready to cope with objections because unless they're panting to buy, they'll have an objection. In almost all sales situations, only about ten objections come up. This means it's a manageable problem; simply prepare a persuasive response for each one.

Here are two techniques that often are helpful.

(a) Repeat the objection "so I understand what you're saying." Usually make it sound worse.

For example:

Customer: "Your price is too high."

Response: "Just so I understand what you're saying, you believe my price is way too high. Is that what you're thinking?"

Customer's answer: "Oh, I wouldn't go so far as to say it's *way* too high."

Then you ask, "How much too high?"

(b) Describe how someone similar to the prospect benefited from your product or service. Often this is an effective way to dispel objections.

THE TEN COMMON OBJECTIONS:

1. It's not in the budget.
2. I have to clear it with someone — my spouse, my partner, my boss (may be the same person) the purchasing agent, the committee, the entire membership.
3. Your price is too high.
4. I want to think about it.
5. I (we) don't have the money.
6. I'm not interested.
7. This is not the right time.
8. I want to shop around.
9. It's too early.
10. It's too late.

Of course people use different words but if you pay close attention, you'll see which common one they're putting forth.

Sit down with your laptop or paper and pen and list the objections you usually encounter. Your list of ten or a dozen common ones will probably differ somewhat from those given above. One of the most effective ways you can increase your sales is to study the objections you usually encounter.

Step 6 — Close the sale

A tremendous amount of stuff is available on closing the sale. About sixty years ago, J. Douglas Edwards came out with an audiotape on closing: a classic and first in its field. Edwards sold so many copies of his tape that he was able to retire in style. Since then there has been a steady flow of books and tapes on closing.

If you are intrigued by Dottie Walters' methods, keep in mind that she sold her benefits to her customers so well that closing was simply a matter of writing the orders. Hard-sell is a dinosaur skeleton in a museum.

One final point: Follow your sales system until you see that the customer is ready to buy, then shut up and write the order. If you keep babbling on and on when your prospects are ready to buy, you will talk some of them out of buying. Happens all the time. Be sensitive to your customer's mood.

The Tenuous but often Tight Connection between Giveaways and Higher Fees

Dottie based her selling philosophy on the concept of giving great value at a price that rewarded the provider handsomely. She often urged individual speakers to raise their fees when she realized, even before they did, that their level of expertise justified it.

She also saw that giveaways have great power to influence possible future buyers. The more buyers one has for one's services or products, the higher are the fees that can be earned. In today's global economy, competition has risen to greater intensity in every field. This means that everyone's search for customers must be more relentless — and especially more efficient — than ever before. In the information industry, the product, if packaged as a download, can be distributed free at no cost. This makes it an ideal medium for turning leads into prospects on their way to becoming customers.

The Formula You've Got to Beat

1. Contacting ten leads gets you one suspect (a person who could conceivably buy).
2. Contacting ten suspects turns up one prospect (a person who clearly would benefit from your product/service and appears able to pay for it).
3. Working with ten prospects yields one sale.

1 x 2 x 3 = 1 in 1,000. Disaster.

If your numbers even begin to look like this formula, analyze your sales system. Find the weakest point, and concentrate on strengthening it. For example, you may need higher quality leads. Your benefits script may need revision. Your pricing structure may need to reflect market conditions more closely. The overall competitiveness of your product/service may need a drastic overhaul. Find what's broke and fix it.

The Dottie Walters Helping Hands Award

In a move typical of her enduring personal drive to help others, Dottie created *The Dottie Walters Helping Hands Award* in 1998 to recognize outstanding helpfulness in the field of professional speaking. It is presented annually by the International Association of Speakers Bureaus (IASB).

The recipients to date are:

1998	Brad Plumb
1999	Deborah Lilly
2000	Claire Carter
2001	Leanne Christie
2002	Jo Cavendor
2003	Nancy Lauterbach
2004	Renee Strom
2005	Jim Chism
2006	No recipient
2007	Scott Chesson

JAMES D. MONTOYA, CAE, EXECUTIVE VICE PRESIDENT • IASB • 7150 WINTON DRIVE SUITE 300 INDIANAPOLIS, IN 46268 • VOICE 317.328.7790 • FAX 317.280.8527 • WWW.IASBWEB.ORG • JIM@IASBWEB.ORG

The secret of joy in work is contained in one word: excellence. To know how to do something well is to enjoy it.

—Pearl Buck

Keeping Up with Today's Information Overload

· Five Steps to Getting the Information You Need Faster: · Read Dynamically · Be Relentlessly Selective · Apply the Quality Test · Subscribe to Summary Services · Seek the Best Possible Understanding of the Big Picture · The Greatest Waste of Time and Energy ·

Studies have revealed many curious facts. Two examples: (A) Upwardly mobile people are considerably less likely to feel overburdened in any area of life than are the less ambitious. (B) Most average performers work harder — that is, put in longer hours — than do more successful people. Yet the day is twenty-four hours long for everyone. Where do the ambitious find the time to do all they do? How did Dottie Walters find the time to create and build her businesses, write her books and give countless speeches and seminars? She did all that, and yet many of those who came in contact with her personally or on the phone were impressed by how relaxed and unhurried she was.

She was well organized, tightly focused, and she enjoyed what she was doing. If we define working as *being paid to do something when you'd rather be doing something else,* then Dottie never worked after she began speaking in public. She was doing what she most enjoyed doing. It wasn't work; it was fun.

Doing what you're passionate about is the greatest form of success.

We can be sure that — except for a rare bit of relaxation now and then — Dottie didn't lose much time to the worst destroyer of useful hours the world has ever seen: TV. Happily, this monster has passed its peak as more and more people opt for interactive activities such as surfing the web, playing video games and outdoor exercise.

What does this have to do with keeping up with today's information overload? Keeping up takes time; the quickest way to gain time is to cut down on your unproductive use of it.

Five Steps to Getting the Information You Need Faster

1. The challenge is to extract the minuscule amount of pure gold you need from the countless tons of worthless overburden — and to do it quickly. This is a vital skill for a public speaker, and for all others who must stay current with activities and developments in their field.

Read Dynamically

The best speed-reading course is Evelyn Wood Reading Dynamics. As one of the authors (Jamison) can testify, this course will enable you to boost your reading speed — *with increased comprehension and recall* — from the average range of 200 to 700 words a minute to a range of 3,000 to 6,000 words a minute — or even more. It sounds incredible, but it's true. To read at the higher speeds, you must learn how to turn pages really fast. At Reading Dynamics, the first lesson is a drill on this simple but essential technique.

Reading fiction at speeds above 3,000 words a minute means that you see the story as a movie. However, it takes more concentration than your untrained slow pace does.

Many people find they can read all kinds of nonfiction — articles in magazines, office memos, business correspondence, biographies, histories, current events and philosophical treatises — at very high speed after mastering the Reading Dynamics method. Technical material related to a particular technology or subject can be assimilated at astonishing speeds by people skilled and knowledgeable in that technology or subject. Reading Dynamics enables anyone to acquire such information far more quickly than can the untrained reader.

Be Relentlessly Selective

If you face an information overload (and who doesn't?) your first step toward managing your time better is to plan how you can avoid exposure to information you don't need. Look no further than the table of contents in books and magazines unless you see a chapter or article that really interests you. Read just that and skip the rest.

Apply the Quality Test

Apply the quality test to everything you might be tempted to read, listen to or watch. You can't study every bit of information that comes your way or may turn up during research. Accept the fact that you'll usually have to make decisions based on imperfect data.

Subscribe to Summary Services

Consider subscribing to services that summarize books in your areas of special interest if you don't want to take a training course to read faster. Experiment with book summaries, weigh what your time is worth against their cost of summaries. For more information, Google search *Executive Summaries* or *Book Summaries.*

Seek the Best Possible Understanding of the Big Picture

No matter what field you work in, it's heavily affected by changes in the world around you. Keep yourself on track by knowing what the most powerful changes that are developing in the world beyond your niche. Many authors put years into researching and distilling their insights into worldwide trends so you can conveniently read them in a book.

Take full advantage of that fact. Read the vital books that make it easier to understand what's really happening in the world in the 21st century's first decade and what's most likely to happen in the second and third decades — or in the entire first half.

Speakers searching for a powerful topic can develop many of them from the vast storehouse of information in dozens of thought-provoking and mind-expanding books. Here is a small sample:

—Anderson, Chris, *The Long Tail*

Discusses why most companies must sell less of more to survive.

—Friedman, Thomas L., *The World Is Flat: A Brief History of the 21st Century.*

Friedman makes a powerful case that America must drastically improve education to stay competitive in the flat world this planet has become. Already China and India confer far more engineering and science degrees on the students pouring out of their universities than American universities do. The problem is not with our universities; it is with the complacency and sense of entitlement that pervades our society. If we shift cultural gears and regain our competitiveness, our nation will benefit enormously from the irresistible march of globalization. If we fail to meet this challenge, we will become mired in third-world poverty before this century is half over.

—Gladwell, Malcolm, *Blink: The Power of Thinking Without Thinking*

Gladwell demonstrates why our gut feelings so often hit the bull's-eye.

The Worst Waste of Time and Energy – Worrying about Things You Can't Control or Influence

Why does the media put so much effort into endlessly discussing all kinds of disasters, present and future? Because fear, pain, suffering and possible catastrophe bring in more revenue than good news will — or so the media seems to believe.

It's hard to avoid getting concerned about newsy fears — tsunamis, hurricanes, rogue waves, asteroid collisions, terrorist attacks, tornadoes, earthquakes, forest fires, volcanic eruptions — few of which will impact you and your loved ones even if they actually happen.

However, if you live on a hurricane coast, near a volcano or in a tinderbox forest, rethink your situation. Guard against complacency and prepare to cope with the special dangers you and your family face. Otherwise, train yourself to reject thinking about any danger outside your primary interests: family, faith, occupation — and the preservation of our planet's fragile eco-system.

People are like stained-glass windows.
They sparkle and shine when the sun is out,
but when the darkness sets in,
their true beauty is revealed only if there is a light from within.

——ELIZABETH KUBLER-ROSS

Did Life Give You a Limo or a Lemon?

· TOUGH STARTS · RAY CHARLES AND STEVIE WONDER · ERIK WEIHENMAYER · TERRY HAFFNER ·

At times, many of us have felt that we got the lemon instead of the limousine. This display of ingratitude insults God's plan for us. You have great talents. You also have wonderful opportunities. Recognize them; think how you can achieve them. Then act. Do something every day, as much as you can but at least take some action toward achieving your next goal.

Tough Starts

Dottie's climb to financial success was launched in desperation and sustained by long hours of hard work that continued for years. It was a tough start — admirable and inspiring. Unfortunately — or perhaps fortunately because overcoming problems brings out the best in us — going through difficult times at some point in their lives is the fate of most people. Yet all of us who were born without physical disabilities have an easy time making our mark compared to those who had to conquer disabilities of the most serious kind.

Everyone who feels inadequate, underprivileged or discouraged should be inspired by the tremendous successes of many who overcame great physical challenges. That inspiration should lead you to set higher goals for yourself and to work smarter and harder to achieve them.

Certainly Dottie recognized her opportunities, acted on them and achieved her initial goals. Then she set higher goals, always higher goals, and generally achieved them. She drew her inspiration from the great minds of the past and present. You can do the same. And don't overlook the people who overcame difficulties far more serious than any the physically fit face. Instead of turning away from them, consider what they achieved, and what their lives would be like if they hadn't pulled themselves out of despair and paid the price to be successful. Why should you do less with your only life?

You must have the adventurous daring to accept yourself as a bundle of possibilities and undertake the most interesting game in the world — making the most of one's best.

——Harry Emerson Fosdick

Ray Charles and Stevie Wonder

Consider Ray Charles and Stevie Wonder. Both of them overcame blindness to achieve great success as entertainers.

Equally inspiring are the achievements of people such as Erik Weihenmayer and Terry Haffner. Both are Americans with very different physical problems and achievements.

Erik Weihenmayer

On May 25, 2001, Erik Weihenmayer stood on the summit of the world's highest peak. Except for one thing, this would hardly be a noteworthy feat in this age of guided tours to the top of Mt. Everest. Here's that one thing: Erik is blind. In fact, he is the first blind person in history to reach the world's most famous summit. A little more than a year later, he summited Mt. Kosciusko in Australia and completed his seven-year quest to climb the Seven Summits — the highest mountains on each of the seven continents. Fewer than one hundred mountaineers have accomplished that feat.

Imagine the incredible determination and raw courage it took to climb mountains by feel, where a single misstep can plummet you down thousands of feet to certain oblivion.

Terry Haffner

Terry Haffner was born with partial legs and no arms but also with an indomitable spirit and a deep commitment to inspire other people to rise above and defeat whatever difficulties they face. In churches, convention centers and schools throughout America, audiences have laughed, cried and been inspired by hearing Terry.

Loving parents, grandparents, doctors and teachers combined with Terry's unyielding faith launched his can-do life. It began early when he accepted God's blueprint for him, accepted all its hurdles and disappointments and began balancing them with small victories that grew into large ones.

His irrepressible spirit and firm focus took him through a Christian high school and enabled him to earn a degree at Purdue University. News stories about Terry's accomplishments opened doors for him so that he could earn a living as a public speaker. His paintings also began to sell after being displayed in many museums, galleries, homes and offices. His growing position as one of Indiana's most treasured painters has increased prices for his works.

Terry's signature message is titled, *When Every Challenge is Tougher, Every Victory Is Sweeter.* Terry's humor, spirit and warmth have touched audiences of every size nationwide. In his public appearances and on canvas, Terry Haffner has enriched countless lives by inviting and inspiring everyone to use all their human riches to the fullest. Terry drives himself around in a sporty red van and has long lived an independent life.

TERRYHAFFNERARTS@YAHOO.COM · 260.416.0161 · 712 OAK TREE COURT, FORT WAYNE, INDIANA · 46845

Undertake something that is difficult; it will do you good. Unless you try to do something beyond what you have already mastered, you will never grow.

—Ronald E. Osborn

If you want something you've never had, do something you've never done.

—James Amps III

A Lifetime of Sharing and Selling Told in Dottie's Own Words

· The How and Why I Got Started · What Can I Do? · The Two Kids, the Baby Stroller and Me · My First Steps · The Hospitality Hostess Service Was Born · Turn on Your Own Selling Power ·

No one will ever tell Dottie's story better than she did. Although Dottie has gone to a better world, her words — in books, audio courses and E-books — remain as an enduring tribute to a remarkable woman. When she came of age, the slow and difficult march of women toward equality of opportunity was just beginning to show important results.

Dottie's impact on speeding this process was immense. Her numerous appearances on many of the major TV programs of the day delivered a powerful message: a woman with little money could create a business almost out of thin air — and make it highly profitable. The Dottie effect of her appearances cannot be measured but, unquestionably, it was profound.

TV appearances were not her only contribution to opening more opportunities for women. A few years after her breakout at the Baldwin Park Bulletin, she wrote her first book, *Never Underestimate the Selling Power of a Woman*. Being the world's first book for saleswomen written by a woman, it was an instant best-seller. By the time she wrote the book, she had already trained thousands of saleswomen. This enabled them to make a good living — a first for many. She continued to train thousands more for the rest of her life. She trained hundreds *after* she hired them for her *Hospitality Hostess Service*. Now, in Dottie's own words:

The How and Why I Got Started

One night in 1948, Bob, my husband, brought home devastating news: "Dottie, I've been hoping things would get better but . . . well, the plant is in trouble. We're behind on the payments and it looks like we should shut down."

I was stunned. The dry cleaning business had seemed so right for Bob. But I could see what had happened. With his happy-go-lucky disposition, Bob hadn't told me the bad news because he was so long recognizing it himself.

We talked all through dinner, searching for a way out. The worst part was my aunt. We'd borrowed $5,000 from her to buy the plant and this obligation had to be repaid. Actually, if we did close down, we'd never be able to pay her back. Then we were getting farther and farther behind on our payments. It was only a question of time before we'd lose our first real home, our car and our furniture.

Also, business conditions were a little rough. Nobody would admit it but the country was in a slump — not only was business slow but jobs were hard to find.

"Honey, can you hold on for another month?" I finally asked Bob. "Maybe things will look up. Or at least we'll have time to think of something!"

"I'll try, Dottie," he said and then went off to bed, a very tired and discouraged man.

I looked around our tiny GI tract home, one like a hundred others in our development, but still full of the personal touches of pride I'd so lovingly given it. I looked at the round, rosy cheeks of our two babies while I read them a bedtime story. Mike was just two and already covered with freckles, topped by red hair. Jeanine was one and as yet not too steady on her chubby legs.

I took a look at myself too after putting the kids to bed. Twenty-three years old, just a high school education, no special training or talents.

What Can I Do?

And yet that night I asked myself a big question: What can I do to help Bob? I felt I had to *do* something no matter how small and insignificant. When you know your husband is down at this business fighting against bankruptcy you can't sit by idly. So I started to look for work.

The next two weeks were discouraging. First, I thought of taking care of other children in my home. They'd be good company for my toddlers and a bit of income for me. I ran an ad but got no answers. Then I heard about a ceramics factory which employed women to paint pieces in their homes. When I got to their door a huge "Closed" sign stared back at me. Could I color photographs? "Sorry, no help needed." Could I clerk in a store? "Sorry, business is so poor we've laid off many of our employees."

Finally, I talked a coffee shop into letting me wash dishes for them during their lunch hour. But after one day the owner said he couldn't use me for another week. My mother had always taught me that "All work is noble and blessed," but I realized I'd have to work with my mind instead of my back if I wanted to achieve the first goal I'd set for myself — our house payment.

That night I couldn't sleep. I kept asking myself why nothing had opened up for me. I put on the coffee pot and sat alone in the quiet house — my family was fast asleep. If only I could do one thing well. What had I ever done that I enjoyed, that seemed to fall my way?

Suddenly I remembered Miss Pettifer, my high school English teacher, who'd had so much faith in my writing ability that I'd become feature editor of *The Alhambra Moor,* our school newspaper.

During my senior year I was made advertising manager of *The Moor.* The owner of a charming dress shop in Alhambra liked my jingles so much she asked me to write a shopper's column for her instead of a regular display ad. This fired my teenage imagination and I worked the rest of the day composing it. When my mother and I were very poor, we'd gone window shopping and we used to tell one another: "We're window-wishing." My maiden name was Wells so I called my column "Window Wishing with Wells." It was quite a success.

But all this had been many years ago. I told myself that night, with housework and babies filling every moment since. Also, what is termed "brilliant" in high school often produces a "ho-hum" in the adult business world. No, I'd have to think of something else. And quickly too because our creditors were beginning to use frightening words like "foreclosure" and "repossession."

It was early morning when I went to bed. I had exhausted all my human resources and so, in searching humility, I turned to prayer. I simply asked God, "What can I do?" Our need was desperate; I was willing and able but I needed the answer to *how* to go about it.

And then, suddenly and quite sharply, two biblical stories I'd first heard at the Methodist Church Sunday school came back to me.

The first was a story of the widow in II Kings who, despairing of losing her two sons into slavery, asked the prophet Elisha, "What can

I do?" She didn't ask him what he could do for her. She didn't ask who else could help her. She was ready to help herself.

And Elisha said, "Tell me, what hast thou in the house?"

And she said, "Thine handmaid hath not any thing in the house, save a pot of oil." She might have said, "I have nothing," but no one has nothing. She scored on two points: first, she was ready to help herself and second, she recognized something of value which was already hers — little though it was.

Elisha told her to go out, borrow vessels from her neighbors, and fill them with her oil.

I could well imagine how she felt. How could she possibly fill many vessels from the little bit of oil she had? But she didn't stop to doubt but filled so many vessels her son couldn't find any more to bring her. Then she went back to the prophet and he said, "Go, sell the oil, and pay the debt and live thou and thy children of the rest."

I thought about this story and then I asked myself, "What do I have in the house to sell?" It didn't necessarily have to be tangible like the widow's oil but it might be some service I could give.

The other biblical story that came to me was the story of the talents in the Book of Matthew. The men who had been given many talents went out into the world and multiplied them but the poor man who was given only one talent had hidden it in the earth. And God took that talent away and gave it to a man who already had ten talents.

Mathew ends the parable by saying, "For unto every one that hath shall be given, and he shall have abundance; but from him that hath not shall be taken away, even that which he hath."

This was a stern lesson and it made me realize that even if I had one small talent I had an obligation to use it — right now.

I jumped out of bed. Could my small talent, my shopper's column from high school days, be my "little oil in the house?" I slipped into my robe, tiptoed into the kitchen and turned on the old, faithful coffee pot again.

In the waste basket beside the stove was a copy of the *Baldwin Park Bulletin,* our weekly newspaper. I pulled it out, spread it open on the kitchen table and carefully read every advertisement.

Then I took a piece of typing paper, rolled it into my mother's typewriter, which I'd borrowed to write letters, and wrote across the top of that clean, white sheet: WINDOW WISHING.

Then painstakingly, I wrote up a sample shopper's column — making it just as eye-catching as I could. I finished at dawn.

The Two Kids, the Baby Stroller and Me

That morning after Bob left for work, I dressed up in my best clothes, dressed the children in their best, put them in the baby stroller — Jeanine riding in the seat, Mike hanging on behind — and walked two miles downtown to the newspaper office.

I almost panicked in front of the heavy oak door to the *Bulletin.* I could hear the big presses in the back pounding rhythmically, but they couldn't compete with my hammering heart. What was I going to say? Did I look business-like pushing two babies in front of me?

I took my sample column out of my purse. I thought about Bob's business, of the delinquent payments and our real need and I pushed my way into the office.

An older, important-looking grey-haired woman glanced up from her desk. "Yes?"

I cleared my throat and tried to speak. Not a sound came out.

Mike said, "Mommy, I wanna go ho . . . me!"

I swallowed and blurted out, "I would like to work for your newspaper.

The lady laughed, "My dear child, we don't need any help here. You haven't a chance." With that she turned back to the papers on her desk.

Just then a small, thin, worried-looking man came through the inner door of the office.

"Sir," I blurted out, "are you the publisher? Because if you are, I want to buy an ad."

He stopped, smiled tiredly at me. "Yes, I'm Charles Heacock, the publisher. But the classified department is over there."

"No," Mr. Heacock," I pushed my sample column toward him. I want to talk to you about buying display space. Every week. I would like to have two columns across, full length."

I was succeeding. I could tell by the interest in his eyes. After all, Mr. Heacock earned his living by selling ads. The one person he couldn't possibly turn down was someone buying space.

I would make a good bargain for him too. A bargain is like an evenly balanced scale — good for both sides. But I would weight his side of the bargain with benefits. I'd make the deal so attractive he wouldn't be able to refuse me. Now I had my answer. I would be *his* customer.

But just then Mrs. Ready, the grey-haired lady, spoke up. "This girl doesn't want to buy space at all. She's looking for work and I've already told her we can't use her."

My heart sank. But Mr. Heacock called into the back room. "Randy, can you come up here for a moment?" George Randolph, the advertising manager, joined us.

"All right," Mr. Heacock said kindly. "Just what do you have in mind?"

I poured out my plan. I'd buy their space for my "Window Wishing" shoppers' column and then resell it for a little more than I paid for it — the difference would be my profit.

"I'll turn in my copy early on Monday," I rushed on eagerly, "so the linotype operator can set it before rush time. And I'll proofread my own copy. And I'll use little cartoons with each paragraph but I'll clip out my own mats. And if I'll be in the way, why I'll come in and work at night or on Sunday. But please, Mr. Heacock, sell me the space!"

By now they were grinning at me. I'd tipped the scales of the bargain in their favor and they couldn't refuse me. Even Mrs. Ready said, "And I thought you wanted a *job!*"

"Okay," Mr. Heacock said, "come back tomorrow and we'll work it out — if you're really willing to work for yourself."

Oh I was. And tomorrow I'd ask him to give me a week's credit so I could start my first column. I could do it. I knew I could.

Right now I smiled and left fast — before they could see tears of gratitude in my eyes. I'd work, all right. I'd use my one tiny talent and maybe — just maybe — it'd grow and multiply. Pushing the children back home that day I didn't know it but I'd just made the most important sale of my life!

My First Steps

The next morning I was out calling on stores in Baldwin Park, selling paragraphs in my column.

"Good luck, Dottie," Bob had said that morning. "Have a big day!"

"Good luck to you too, honey," I said and watched him go off to the plant. His morale was higher and we were still hoping the dry cleaning business would pick up.

I'd dressed myself, Mike and Jeanine carefully and walked the two miles again, pushing the stroller along. One wheel was bad and it made the funniest ka-plop-pa noise. I found it was easy to rehearse what I was going to say to the merchants with this rhythm as a background,

I always tried to smile as I talked, even when they said no — which was often. And I confined myself to a two-block territory — the heart of town. My first ad was taken by a photographer, the next from a jeweler, then followed by a shoe store, a hardware store, even the restaurant where I'd washed dishes.

I did restrict their ads to one time each on their first order to be sure they weren't buying out of sympathy for me.

"I'll come back and sell you another ad if you get results," I promised them.

Often I got overly enthusiastic and wrote too many words into their paragraph so I only made a few pennies on their ads. But with most of them I cleared a dollar on each ad. The 20 spaces cost me $2 and I charged $3 so that, when I sold all the spaces, I could earn $20 a week — just double what the dishwashing job had paid!

Soon Bob and I were able to send off our house payment, then our car payment for, quite wonderfully, his business had picked up a little. Working was such fun! I was taking care of my customers even if the day left me exhausted. Often Bob worked late and would come home to find me reading the kids their bedtime story with my feet in a tub of hot water.

"What a sight," he'd say. "Do you still think you're working with your *mind*?"

I didn't have an answer for that one.

I was learning a good deal about selling — all the hard way, of course. But this very fact made me learn each lesson well. After all, I told myself when I got discouraged, I can't afford *not* to learn.

The next three months I worked hard on my column until, by the time fall rolled around I was netting $80 a month. I was beginning to put cardboard soles in my shoes to increase my mileage. But at last I could afford a baby sitter and it was so much better for my children to run and shout and play in their own backyard. I was grateful when my neighbors were so quick to offer their help. With my mind free of worry about Mike and Jeanine, I could make my rounds faster and more cheerfully.

One night Bob came home with a two-door Model A Ford for me.

"The back seat is so big the kids can't fall out," he said with a twinkle in his eyes, "and this'll get the cardboard out of your shoes."

I was touched by his thoughtfulness, but fearful too. "Oh, Bob, we really can't afford it." The $125 seemed like a fortune to me.

"We can't afford not to," he said firmly. "You're going to get sick if you keep this up. Besides, think how you can sell more ads if you aren't spending so much time walking."

I was overjoyed. To me, the Model A was a limousine. Bob had arranged to pay it off in installments and truly I was able to cover more ground on wheels.

The upholstery was ragged and dirty so I sold space to an auto upholstery man and he exchanged his bright red seat covers for my ads. Then Bob painted the wheels red to match and off I went to sell more ads.

Of course, my life was hectic. Every time I'd get down on my hands and knees to scrub the kitchen floor, the telephone would ring with someone asking about an ad. Often I found myself hanging up the wet wash at night with a flashlight shining from my apron pocket.

It was a scramble not to shortchange the children but somehow I managed. When I couldn't be with them, I had lots of games and projects planned for them. The back seat of my car was stocked with toys. And, of course, they had one another. Just a year apart, they were close companions — even if the fight got hot and heavy every once in a while.

There were days when everything seemed to go against me. One afternoon while I was trying to give myself a home permanent some paper bags I'd foolishly stored above the stove caught on fire. In the rush to put it out, I laid the bottle of permanent neutralizer down. When I got back Mike had the bottle in his hand, a look of horror on his face. He'd drunk it!

I rushed him down to the emergency hospital, hair wet, curlered and still not neutralized. An hour later we were back at home and he was fine. I was inspecting my hair to see if it was going to fall out when Bob walked in.

"What's new?" he asked.

This struck me funny. I poured out all that'd happened and then we both laughed so hard we fell into one another's arms.

"Honey," he said, "I don't think this marriage will ever die of boredom."

That was the understatement of our lives!

One day I asked Mr. Heacock for more work. Every little bit helped.

"Okay, Dottie. I'll pay you $1,000 if you sell 1,000 subscriptions for me."

I thought a minute. "You mean a dollar a subscription?"

He nodded.

I thought about all the money we still owed all over town. "I accept your offer," I said. To his amazement, I grabbed a stack of newspapers.

That very afternoon I was out calling on the new houses in town, the new tract developments, wherever I knew I'd find newcomers who wouldn't have had a chance to subscribe to the paper. These people were a very good and reliable source for new, untapped business. Of course, Mr. Heacock had been jesting, but I did sell his 1,000 subscriptions — in the next two years.

Mr. Staples, one of my regular customers, heard about what I was doing. He asked me to sell the newcomers on signing up for his trash pickup service. Then a fence man asked me to pick up sales leads for him.

Hospitality Hostess Service Was Born

One day Mr. Staples stopped by my house and I got out the coffee pot. For my customers are my friends too.

"Listen Dottie," he said, "I think you should start a newcomer welcoming service. You already know all the downtown merchants, don't you?"

I nodded.

"And you're already calling on new move-ins?"

Again I nodded.

"Well, I have a friend who has a welcoming service. I can get all the dope from him. I think it'd be a natural for you. And Dottie, I'll be your first customer."

I was speechless from the impact of his idea. After he left I analyzed it. It sounded good. I knew there was a real need for it in Baldwin Park. We had a lot of tracts going up and newcomers needed an introduction to the city along with an introduction to the products and services of my merchants.

When Bob got home that night he liked the idea too. So with the information from Mr. Staples we thought up a good name — Hospitality Hostess Service. I approached my regular customers with the idea and that first day I signed up fifteen of them. I wasn't prepared for such a positive reaction. Mr. Staples' idea was such a big success I realized I needed help. I couldn't do it all alone.

"Yoo-hoo, anybody home?" It was my neighbor, Virginia Thompson, who'd been so wonderful at checking my faulty spelling on my ads.

I grabbed her in my excitement. "Virginia, how would you like to go in business with me? I blurted out. "We can share the work and the money right down the middle. What do you say?"

Virginia was like an amused big sister. "Dottie, I don't know the first thing about selling or business. But fire away. I'm listening."

We worked day and night. I bought myself a desk for $15 from the Goodwill store; our shelves were orange crates lined with blue paper to match our living room.

I made up a coupon for each merchant's business, then stapled them together in a little book. The coupon offered the newcomer either a welcome gift or so much credit on his first purchase. The object was to get the newcomer to call at the store to get acquainted — a unique form of advertising.

I borrowed a mimeograph machine and Virginia and I tried to print up the coupons. They were a mess. We got more ink on the floor and walls than on the paper.

"Let's talk to Mr. Heacock tomorrow about doing our printing," I finally said, "and call it a day."

"Amen," Virginia said.

We welcomed a hundred new families in January and everyone greeted us warmly. I made half of the hostess calls and kept up my shopper's column. It was hard work and I had to try even harder to be a good wife and mother. But after we paid all our bills at the end of the first month, Virginia and I netted almost $100 each.

One night early in February Virginia and I got together to plan our future. We were lightheaded with ideas and enthusiasm. Her mother, who worked in a dress shop, had sent us two matching brown dresses to wear on our calls. "Just like airline stewardesses," we said, laughing as we tried them on. Everything was coming our way; it was a miracle. We said goodnight early and Virginia went home.

The next morning the telephone awakened me at 7:30. It was another neighbor. "Dottie, Virginia is dead. She died of a cerebral hemorrhage during the night."

All that day I walked around, numb with shock. My enthusiasm, my resources deserted me. I could not think of one single uplifting thought. I could only think about Virginia's husband and two little boys — left alone. I went to their home, did what I could and left, feeling more helpless than ever.

That night, Virginia's husband, almost speechless with grief, sat in our living room. Bob and I looked at one another helplessly. What could we do? What could we say?

Finally he began to talk. "I hate to ask you . . . but I haven't any money . . . the funeral, you know. Dottie and Bob . . . could you come up with some cash to cover Virginia's share of the Hostess Service? Say about $400?" Then he put his head down in his hands.

Our hearts ached for him and his two little boys. "We'll find it somehow," I heard Bob tell him.

After he'd left Bob said, "At a time like this there isn't much most people can do. But this time we can help."

So we did. We borrowed the money, not from Mr. Heacock, who was quick to offer it, but from the bank. We had to be honest with the banker. We were deep in debt; Bob still wasn't able to bring anything home but we promised we'd repay it somehow. We got the loan on our signature and had the cashier's check made out to Mr. Thompson.

Walking out of the bank, I suddenly felt very tired and alone. My friend was gone. All the responsibility of the Hostess Service and the

"Window Wishing" column was on my shoulders. If I don't make a go of them, I asked myself, how can we ever make it?

But Bob had said, "At a time like this, there isn't much most people can do. But this time we can help."

That's the way I felt as I handed the check to Virginia's husband. The next day we buried her in the new brown dress.

That night I came slowly out of my paralyzed state when a quotation from Epictetus came to me. I ran to the book of his *Discourses* where years before I'd marked the passage. It read:

> *When you have closed your doors and darkened your room, remember never to say that you are alone, for you are not alone. God is within and your genius is within — and what need have they of light to see what you are doing?*
>
> ——*Epictetus*

Those words from the ancient sage inspired me.

Turn on Your Own Selling Power

By the end of the week after Virginia's death I knew I'd have to decide between the Hostess Service and the shopper's column. I couldn't handle both by myself. I chose the Hostess Service.

That next year I alone made 1,000 calls. Then I began training my neighbors to make calls and sell the merchants on becoming our sponsors. Some of them started out baby sitting and answering the phone. One day I saw Gene Brown take down a message in shorthand; I made her my secretary. Janet Nakada, Lorna Taylor and Rhoda Weisz all started sorting, stapling and baby sitting. We began to grow. And grow.

Today, 13 years later, (written circa 1970) Gene is still my secretary, Lorna my bookkeeper and Janet and Rhoda help run the office. But our office is ten times the size of our old dining room. Instead of 15 advertisers, we have 1,500. My two-block territory has expanded to 68 Southern California cities where 124 hostesses make approximately 3,000 calls each month. Through the years I've personally trained hundreds of women to sell.

After we paid back my aunt, Bob was finally able to sell the cleaning plant. Now he operates our own print shop where he does regular printing jobs as well as our coupon books. It is hectic now (circa 1960) most of the time but we have fun. We are all working together toward our future. Sometimes when we get rushed, I recruit Mike and Jeanine to sort coupons until we can all go home to dinner together.

It's been a good life; hard work has taught us a world of wisdom. I've learned how to sell through trial and error; Bob has learned the printing business in the same way.

All my life, I always wanted to be somebody.
Now I see that I should have been more specific.

——Lily Tomlin

The wise see more from the bottom of a well
than fools can from a mountain top.

——Harriet Tubman

Focus Humankind's Greatest Minds on Boosting Your Career

· How to Open the Bulging Treasury House of Existing Wisdom · Dottie's Master's Course at Bastiat Free University · Benjamin Franklin · Albert Einstein · Socrates · Plato · Aristotle · Epictitus ·

How to Open the Bulging File of Existing Wisdom

Some of them passed away thousands of years ago, but still their words echo across the intervening centuries or millennia with all their original vigor and enchantment. All it takes to co-opt the great minds into enhancing your earning potential is to drink in their words. Read them. They are easy to find in any public library, easy to own for small sums in any bookstore. If you can spare more time than money, search the used book stores in your area and on the Internet.

What can we learn from Dottie's life to raise our own results and happiness to higher levels? In a short period of time Dottie leapt from being a sheltered homemaker and mother to become a highly successful entrepreneur. Remember, she began doing this more than half a century ago at a time when few women even attempted to play such a role. What made her get out of the house and earn money, but also to figure out how to start with no money?

The answer is that she had long sought wisdom. While still in high school she became fascinated by the vast wealth of knowledge available at school and public libraries. Best of all — considering her limited resources at the time — it was all free. So, at a young age she began reading what the world's deepest thinkers had given the world. Unconsciously, she began doing what Ed McMahon was later to urge on people who aspire to stardom: "When your big chance comes, *be ready!*"

Dottie's Master's Course at Bastiat Free University

You may think that you'll quickly forget what you read, or feel that it will be heavy going. To counter this, start by reading only what you enjoy in the world's greatest books. A strong move in this direction would be to take Dottie's master's course at Bastiat Free University. It's called *Finding Entrepreneurial Success.* It's not based on the books she wrote, but rather on the books that had a positive influence on her life. Dottie supplied the following book list, saying: "I am an avid reader, but will give you just a few of the most influential books I have ever read."

1. *The Power Of Positive Thinking* by Dr. Norman Vincent Peale
2. *We Got Fired!* by Harvey Mackay
3. *The Autobiography Of Benjamin Franklin*
4. The Autobiographical Books By Amelia Earhart
    - *The Price Of Courage*
    - *Legends Of Air Power*
    - *Heroines Of The Sky*
5. Anything by Albert Einstein, including:
    - *The World As I See It*
    - *Ideas & Opinions*
6. *The Law Of Success* by Napoleon Hill.

Benjamin Franklin

God grant that not only the love of liberty but a thorough knowledge of the rights of man pervade all the nations of the earth, so that a philosopher may set his foot anywhere on its surface and say: "This is my country."

——Benjamin Franklin

One of Dottie's top sources of useful insights was Benjamin Franklin. His fame, and the high regard Americans have for him more than two centuries after he passed from the scene is amply demonstrated by the 902 books by and about him that are readily available today.

Franklin worked hard at writing homely, down-to-earth advice for gaining prosperity and living a long and useful life. His *Poor Richard's Almanac*, an enduring bestseller in its day, shared its wisdom by humorously urging thrift and industry on Americans in the English Colonies that became the United States.

Benjamin Franklin didn't claim that all the wisdom he poured into *Poor Richard's Almanac* had originated with him. He attributed much of it to age-old sources: The Bible, Plato, Epictitus among others. Dottie did the same thing, never claiming that her wonderful insights sprang from her own mind. Insight leads to action, which was Dottie's greatest strength.

What distinguishes outstanding people such as Dottie Walters from those of us who play a supporting, rather than a starring, role in life?

Part of the explanation lies among such qualities as courage, motivation, determination, intelligence, discipline, decisiveness, self-confidence and persistence. But how does one learn to be more courageous, more highly motivated, more determined, and all the rest? Most importantly, what can we learn from Dottie's life to boost our own results and happiness?

Albert Einstein

The solution is at hand.

——*Albert Einstein*

Dottie never suggested that she had more than a hazy idea of what Albert Einstein's theories about Relativity are. But, knowing him to be a down-to-earth guy who had a lot of sound ideas about meeting life's challenges, she decided early on to see what Einstein could teach her. She checked out Einstein books at her local library, read them, and learned solutions to problems she would face later. Einstein didn't disappoint her. He was at the height of his fame when Dottie reached adulthood and World War II broke over the world. Now, half a century after Einstein's death, Amazon offers 325 titles by or about him.

But Dottie didn't stop with gleaning knowledge from Einstein. She sought out all the best known great minds, from ancient Greeks and Romans to America's Founding Fathers and on to contemporary thinkers.

Read the wisdom that humankind's most innovative minds have conveniently packaged for everyone. Access is cost free at any public library, or nominal at your favorite bookstore.

Socrates, Plato, Aristotle

The three great thinkers of ancient Athens continue to influence on Western thought after more than 2,300 years. Socrates divided reality into two irreconcilable domains: the material and the spiritual. This concept has been of incalculable influence in the history of Western philosophy and religion.

Socrates:

All men's souls are immortal, but the souls of the righteous are immortal and divine.

Our prayers should be for blessings in general, for God knows best what is good for us.

The end of life is to be like God, and the soul following God will be like Him.

By all means marry. If you get a good wife, you'll be happy. If you get a bad one, you'll become a philosopher and that is a good thing for any man.

Employ your time in improving yourself by other men's writings, so that you shall gain easily what others have labored hard for.

If all misfortunes were laid in one common heap whence everyone must take an equal portion, most people would be contented to take their own and depart.

Once made equal to man, woman becomes his superior.

One who is injured ought not to return the injury, for on no account can it be right to do an injustice; and it is not right to return an injury, or to do evil to any man, however much we have suffered from him.

The greatest way to live with honor in this world is to be what we pretend to be.

Plato:

The unexamined life is not worth living.

The way to gain a good reputation is to endeavor to be what you desire to appear.

True wisdom comes to each of us when we realize how little we understand about life, ourselves, and the world around us.

We are what we repeatedly do. Excellence, then, is a habit..

Wisdom begins in wonder.

Worthless people live only to eat and drink; people of worth eat and drink only to live

There must always remain something that is antagonistic to good.

Aristotle:

Sometimes the ancient Greeks startle us with how sharply their comments apply to today, when the scramble to choose the next occupant of the White House intensifies as 2007 winds down:

A tyrant must put on the appearance of uncommon devotion to religion. Subjects are less apprehensive of illegal treatment from a ruler whom they consider god-fearing and pious. On the other hand, they less easily move against him, believing that he has the gods on his side.

In making a speech one must study three points: first, the means of producing persuasion; second, the language; third the proper arrangement of the various parts of the speech.

All human actions have one or more of these seven causes: chance, nature, compulsions, habit, reason, passion, desire.

All men by nature desire knowledge.

All paid jobs absorb and degrade the mind.

All virtue is summed up in dealing justly.

Anybody can become angry - that is easy, but to be angry with the right person and to the right degree and at the right time and for the right purpose, and in the right way - that is not within everybody's power and is not easy.

At his best, man is the noblest of all animals; separated from law and justice he is the worst.

Bashfulness is an ornament to youth, but a reproach to old age. Both oligarch and tyrant mistrust the people, and therefore deprive them of their arms.

Bring your desires down to your present means. Increase them only when your increased means permit.

Character may almost be called the most effective means of persuasion.

Courage is the first of human qualities because it is the quality which guarantees the others.

Democracy arises out of the notion that those who are equal in any respect are equal in all respects; because men are equally free, they claim to be absolutely equal.

Democracy is when the indigent, and not the men of property, are the rulers.

Dignity does not consist in possessing honors, but in deserving them.

Education is an ornament in prosperity and a refuge in adversity.

Education is the best provision for old age.

Even when laws have been written down, they ought not always to remain unaltered.

For what is the best choice, for each individual is the highest it is possible for him to achieve.

Happiness depends upon ourselves.

Homer taught all other poets the art of telling lies skillfully.

If liberty and equality, as is thought by some, are chiefly to be found in democracy, they will be best attained when all persons alike share in government to the utmost.

If one way be better than another, that you may be sure is nature's way.

In a democracy the poor will have more power than the rich, because there are more of them, and the will of the majority is supreme.

Epictetus:

Leave your children well instructed rather than rich, for the hopes of the instructed are better than the wealth of the ignorant.

Control your passions lest they take vengeance on you

Difficulties are things that show people what they are.

First learn the meaning of what you say, and then speak.

First say to yourself what you would be; and then do what you have to do.

God has entrusted me with myself.

A wise man does not grieve for things he has not, but rejoices for those he has.

If evil be spoken of you and it be true, correct yourself, if it be a lie, laugh at it.

If you wish to be a writer, write.

Imagine for yourself a character, a model personality, whose example you determine to follow, in private as well as in public.

It is the nature of the wise to resist pleasures; the nature of the foolish to be a slave to them.

It's not what happens to you, but how you react to it that matters..

If you would not be forgotten . . .
Either write things worthy of reading,
Or do things worth the writing.

—Benjamin Franklin

Experiences with Dottie

Wendy Keller · Allan Wallace · Catina Payne · Jack Nichols · Ann Convery · Jack Sims · Sunny Bossenmaier · Tom Marcoux · Jo Condrill · Brian Marinelli · Norma T. Hollis · Bob Bly · Stephanie Chandler · Ross Mackay · Anita Paul Johnston · Andrew John Heath · Ana Tikhomiroff · Michael Levy · Sherry Knight · David Evans · Cynthia Brian · Wajid · Mo Bailey · Eric De Groot · Dawna H. Jones · Carlos Gutierrez · Dr. Jan Yager · Michael Podolinsky · Phillipa Challis · Dr. Bill Clawson · Naomi Rhode, CSP, CPAE · Dr. Reesa Woolf · Terry Tillman · Paul Brosche · Carolyn Cousins-Goldman · Paul Talbot · Avon Drummond · Jacqueline Sidman, Ph.D · Alan Fairweather · Freddie Ravel · Michael Modzelewski ·John Avianantos · Elizabeth Kearney, Ph.D · Paul Lawrence Vann · Dr. Bette Daoust · Rolland E. Proulx · Dell Dorenbosch · Michael Wells · Toni Henderson-Mayers ·

By personal example as well as in her magazine, Dottie gently encouraged others to emulate her devotion to the concept of sharing. In doing so — and perhaps with greater impact with her compelling words of encouragement in her books, at her countless speaking events, and over the phone to those lucky enough to have had that experience — she reached out and touched the hearts of countless people, thousands or hundred of thousands of them. Here and in the next chapter are a few samples of how her students, colleagues, clients, partners and phone contacts, all of whom she considered her friends, used the wisdom and expertise she shared with them.

Wendy Keller:

THE LEGEND OF DOTTIE

I first heard of Dottie years before I met her. I was a young, brash literary agent selling books and had somehow come to represent a few professional speakers. One of them mentioned how Dottie helped him get started and suggested I give her a ring. Something about his gratitude to Dottie struck me, but I never called.

A few years later in 1995, I was coerced into attending a National Speakers Association conference in Irvine, California. I had no intention of attending. I planned to just drop off a publishing colleague. Earlier that day, we'd both been featured speakers at a huge conference in San Diego. But when I walked into the huge ballroom at NSA, to my unfathomable shock, there was that same client on the platform! He was on two gigantic I-mag screens right in front of me!

I signed up for membership a half hour later. I was surprised to come across several of my literary clients present. One of them insisted on introducing me to a petite older woman in a wild hat. She had kind eyes and a mean handshake.

"I'm Dottie Walters," she said.

I introduced myself and Dottie asked me what I do. Within a week of that meeting, she'd invited me come present a program for her symposium. I agreed without hesitation.

When I arrived at the Sheraton Universal hotel for the symposium, I found she'd packed the room full of talented wanna-bes. I did my speech and then watched the "show." I was impressed at the way Dottie managed, coordinated, marketed, pitched, introduced speakers, sold, encouraged and directed things seamlessly, and almost without taking a breath. I sensed her business savvy for the first time that day.

I ended up selling books for five of the attendees that night, becoming friendly with a half dozen new colleagues — the other speakers--most notably Tom Antion, who grew to become famous in his own niche, and Barney Zick. I spent time with my client Raleigh Pinskey, that dynamo of publicity, whose book I had recently placed. I met Ray Cooper who spoke about infomercials. Ray and I began a life-changing friendship that has lasted to this day.

I was invited to speak for Dottie's groups in the future, too. Every time, I met interesting people with passion for what they do. Dottie was always the hub of the experience, the rest of us just spokes. She was the piston that drove the engine. She was the Great Connector. I saw her in a softer mode sometimes, too. On occasion at NSA events, we'd sit and swap motherhood stories or talk about business strategy. She was always ready to strike up a chat, especially if there was a pot of gold at the end of it for her company. Dottie impressed me most with her style — how she combined her pure Scottish focus on profits by folding people into her empire and into her heart. Like all who knew her, our lives were enriched by her example and her personal power.

——WENDY KELLER, SENIOR AGENT, KELLER MEDIA, INC. · LITERARY AGENCY & SPEAKERS BUREAU · QUERY@KELLERMEDIA.COM · HELP@KELLERMEDIA.COM · WWW.KELLERMEDIA.COM · 23852 WEST PACIFIC COAST HIGHWAY, SUITE 701 · MALIBU, CA · 90265 USA · VOICE 310.857.6828 · FAX 310.857.6373

Allan Wallace:

The first time I met Dottie Walters was just after I had finished a speech. Dottie took the time to offer me a helpful critique, and to inquire if I was considering speaking full time. At the time one of Dottie's ventures was publishing. She suggested that I write a chapter for a book she was editing. Yes, Dottie wanted authors, but it was obvious that she was more interested in lending credibility to my speaker's resume than finding another author. One reason Dottie was respected and successful was she worked so hard at helping others be successful.

As an example, Dottie demonstrated understanding of the challenges faced trying to re-engineer higher education. When I started working on the concept for Bastiat Free University, Dottie revealed yet another positive influence on her life to encourage me, and it worked! I will never forget her telling me stories about her Scottish Grandfather.

Dottie Walters is missed. However her motivating influence on the thousands she touched directly will continue. Those that have been inspired by Dottie are now sharing with others. Another magnifying impact of her life are influences such as BFU that are enhanced by her contributions.

—ALLAN WALLACE, RECTOR · BASTIAT FREE UNIVERSITY · SELF-DIRECTED LEARNING FOR VISIONARIES AND ENTREPRENEURS · WWW.SILENTPC.ORG

Catina Payne:

HOW DOTTIE WALTERS IMPACTED MY LIFE

I met Dottie Walters at one of her live seminars in New York City in October 2001. At the time, I was enrolled in a personal coach training program. I wanted to learn from Dottie how I could add public speaking as a profit center for my coaching business. The first thing that struck me about Dottie is how very personable she was. I called her office in California a few weeks before the seminar. I could not believe that I was able to talk with her. The famous Dottie Walters took my phone call! Dottie took time to find out what my goals were and she offered helpful advice.

When we met at the seminar, she was the same in person as over the telephone. It was like I was being taught by an old friend. If things don't turn out the way you plan, don't panic. God has it all under control.

—CATINA PAYNE · CPAYNE@SUFFOLK.LIB.NY.US · 631.643.0891 · WWW.MAXIMUMIMPACTCOACHINGSERVICES.COM · CATINA IS A PERSONAL COACH HELPING PEOPLE REACH THEIR PERSONAL AND PROFESSIONAL POTENTIAL AND LIVE A BALANCED LIFE.

Jack Nichols:

THE DOTTIE WALTERS EFFECT

On a warm summer day, a group gathered around a lady who had just finished speaking to us about how to make money in the speaking profession. I had been speaking for several years, but not as successfully as I would have wanted. So much of what she said made sense. I did not know this lady, but I did know that I wanted to know her. How would I have an opportunity to meet this woman? She was the founder of the organization, the keynote speaker of the meeting and clearly a mentor to most people in the meeting? I felt small in her presence ever, though I was twice her size.

I stood back several feet listening to questions and answers. She noticed me and smiled. After answering more questions and suggesting people read one of her books. She looked at me again, and asked me directly, "What topic do you speak on?" I said, "I speak on many topics." She then said, "What is your main topic?" I had to tell her in so many words that it was motivating people to sell products for a multi level marketing company. She then told me a short story of how she has spoken to many MLM and direct selling companies and that Tupperware gave her one of her biggest breaks. She asked my name and looked me right in the eye and said, "Here is my card, call me and let me help you."

I did not take her up on the offer, but did buy one of her books and skim read it. My world was real busy and my speaking career was growing again. Then the company I spoke for changed owners and I felt disconnected. I was trying to redirect my career and saw Dottie's book on my shelf. Finally, I read it cover to cover. I also called Dottie and went to see her at "the ranch." She met me at the door and took me through the house. She told me about the wild bear that comes from the hills and climbs the tree located in sight of her window. We walked downstairs where there was a collection of books, sayings and pictures, all from or about Benjamin Franklin. Awards were all around us but she did not mention them. We went to her downstairs office and she told me about the ice cream fountain and how it came to be in her home. It was a gift from her husband. We sat and talked for about two hours and as I told her my plans, she would ask me questions and follow up with more questions. She had helped me understand what it took to be in control of my future. I had a lot of work to do, but felt I could do it.

A week later Dottie called me and suggested I take a weekend class she was teaching at her home. I did and that was two days of open-my mind-and-stick-in-my-future all wrapped up with more information than a person could ever really understand. It was the beginning of my new career that included writing, speaking, coaching and training. I understood what I needed to do to market myself and to have Speaker's Bureaus hire me.

Over the years I would meet with Dottie and talked to her on the phone many times. She would call and leave me a quick message just to boost my spirits. I started coaching other speakers and Dottie's books were our textbooks. If the speaker did well they could go meet with Dottie. She was the prize they would earn.

Dottie would ask them the famous question, "What topic do you speak on?" And the answers were never what she wanted to hear. They had read her books but they did not know how to apply the information to themselves. The Dottie Effect would take hold within a few minutes and it was WOW! I knew exactly how they felt.

One exception was when I took a fellow Toastmaster and friend Terri Marie to see Dottie. When Dottie asked her the question, Terri knew exactly what she wanted to do and what topics she wanted to speak on. Terri and Dottie became close friends and shared many interests, including poetry.

My relationship with Dottie turned more personal over the years. I was speaking less and we were mostly interested in how we were personally. Dottie always had a busy schedule; however, she was excited to speak to me. I knew that she would take my calls if she possibly could or call back soon. I felt honored by her interest, and one day I mentioned that I was impressed and in some ways did not feel I deserved such interest. Dottie looked at me and smiled and said, "Jack, you always make me feel so good when we talk. I consider you one of my best friends. Thank you for being in my life." I was confused and honored. How could I be so important to this world-famous woman, speaker to masters in industry, royalty and leaders around the world? I felt she was more then a friend, she was my mentor, as close to a soul mate as we could be.

I asked Dottie to come and speak to our Toastmasters International Speakers' Bureau. The large room was filled with so many people wanting to hear from the grand lady. She was far more than an author, she was a friend to all and she was honored that they wanted to be close to her and hear her stories. It really didn't matter what she said, only that she was there telling us about her children's stroller with the broken wheel, putting cardboard in her shoes, and finally publishing her first book and starting the advertising agency. She was doing what she did so well, leading the way for women and men to find success in life. People left that night invigorated to finish their books or work on their new topic and share their messages. Dottie's stories had an effect on each person in the way they needed to be affected.

Dottie was to be given the lifetime achievement award by the Greater Los Angeles Chapter of the National Speakers Association at the Summer Symposium in Palm Desert, California. I was no longer a member of GLAC/NSA; however, I wanted to be there when Dottie received that honor. This was the organization where I first met Dottie many years before. The day of the event came and Dottie was tired from the long drive and walk from the parking lot. Dottie needed to rest on a bench in the hallway. I found her there and sat with her for a few minutes and then we walked slowly into the room with her holding my arm. She was tired, however the audience did not know. They saw the founder of their chapter stand and deliver as motivational a speech as she had ever given in my presence.

Dottie had donated a complete set of CD's from the Magnificent Marketing Symposium, a four-day complete marketing program for writers, speakers, and trainers. I had attended a past symposium and was willing to auction her CD set with some of the other donated items. It was a lot of fun and I was able to receive a wining bid of $1,500 for an item they could have ordered from Dottie's office for $995. Dottie was excited that so many people wanted that set of CD's. It was a validation to her and the effect she had on so many.

As time came and went, Dottie was unable to drive and missed attending many things including the bimonthly meeting of the Southern California Book Publicists, in Studio City, California. Terri Marie suggested we take Dottie to the meeting. We enjoyed being with her and met many people because we were with Dottie. It was an adventure for the three of us that would end most evenings well past 11 p.m. in Dottie's living room talking about the event. The meetings were interesting, but the drive to and from the meetings was truly fun. Dottie addressed the SCBP meeting and was given a standing ovation and then, only two months later, Dottie was falling asleep halfway through the meeting and we had to leave early. Dottie slept all the way back to her home. Terri and I walked Dottie to her bedroom. I said goodnight and locked the doors on my way out. I closed the driveway gates, just like I always did, but this time was the last time. Dottie passed away a few weeks later on Valentine's Day, so fitting for a person who loved so many for so long.

Now when I am searching for the right answer to a decision, I think of what Dottie would say. I remember the questions and thinking process. It is as if Dottie is right there helping me with my career, just as she had the last twenty years.

—JACK NICHOLS · JACKNICHOLS@DSLEXTREME.COM · 562 531 3990

Ann Convery:

I consulted with Dottie, she taught and inspired me. Dottie's genius, her courage, and her great heart leave a huge legacy. I was so stunned by the fact that she never raised her voice, and yet was able to wheel and deal like the genius she was.

This is from Thornton Wilder's *The Bridge of San Luis Rey*:

> "And we ourselves shall be loved for a while and forgotten. But the love will have been enough; all those impulses of love return to the love that made them. Even memory is not enough for love.
>
> There is a land of the living, and a land of the dead and the bridge is love, the only survival, the only meaning."

—ANN CONVERY · "SPEAK YOUR BUSINESS IN 30 SECONDS OR LESS" · HIGH PERFORMANCE COMMUNICATION SKILLS · 323-644-7955 · ACONVERY@PACBELL.NET

Jack Sims:

When I was a wannabe speaker as part of my due diligence and research, I visited Dottie at her home in Glendale. We had a wonderful time together for a couple of hours and she gave me some wonderful stories and information on how to proceed in the speaking business. However, what I truly remember best are two things that have greatly impacted my career:

1. She told me "Speakers Bureaus are not in the business of growing speakers, they are in the business of growing their Speakers Bureaus."

2. She recommended that I join NSA, and I did.

Both pieces of information have been career changing and I will be forever grateful for them. This is a debt that cannot be repaid!

—JACK SIMS · 914 509 5170 · WWW.JACKSIMS.COM · INFO@JACKSIMS.COM · JACK SPEAKS ON BUSINESS TOPICS SUCH AS "MOST MARKETING STINKS." HE IS THE AUTHOR OF GROWING YOUR BUSINESS INTO A BRAND 2002

Sunny Bossenmaier:

THE MAGIC OF DOTTIE WALTERS

There was something magical about Dottie Walters. The moment I walked into the seminar she was presenting, I knew I was there "for a reason." I thought I had come to get some tips on public speaking and speakers bureaus. I was there helping out friends who wanted to use the information to expand their businesses, but could not attend the seminar personally because of a scheduling conflict. I had no idea I would come away with not only the information needed for my friend, but also information for myself, that was of much greater value for me personally than I ever could imagine.

Dottie was in her senior years when I met her, but I didn't get the impression that she knew that, and within moments, I too had forgotten her age, as I was swept away by her youthful enthusiasm and vibrant presence.

She was down to earth, warm, and inviting, the type of person you instantly took a liking to. I had just gone through a rough and unwanted divorce in which I lost my marriage, my home, my career, and my self-esteem. I found myself middle-aged, on my own, out of work, and struggling. As much as I tried to get back on my feet, the job market and circumstances did not seem in my favor at the time. I could not get my confidence back in myself. I was floundering in life, but not ready or able to admit it. I sat in the seminar ready to take meticulous notes for my friends. I had no idea just how much of a life changing experience meeting Dottie Walters was going to be.

Dottie began the seminar by talking about how she had gotten to where she was in life. The struggles she had gone through, facing debt, struggling to keep her house, and being the one responsible for making ends meet with two small children in tow. She told of how she literally had to start from nothing and take the world in her own hands and create something for herself, from herself.

All of a sudden, I realized Dottie was not just going to be giving me ideas about the world of professional speaking, she was speaking from her heart and experience and using those experiences to give me and others the guidance, confidence and inspiration necessary to face our own lives and our own problems head on. She was giving me the opportunity to make a choice not to become a victim of my past. She reminded me that the only person who could help me was me, and the only way to help myself was to believe in myself and create what I needed to be successful.

I made the decision right then to follow Dottie's lead and inspiring story and become more than I ever had thought I could be. I decided to pull myself up by my boot straps so to speak, to stop waiting for life to happen, and instead start making life happen for myself.

After the seminar, I wrote an email to Dottie explaining how much her words had meant to me, how inspired I was, and how I felt I was "supposed to be there" because she had touched my spirit beyond any way that I felt I could find to thank her. She wrote me back:

> "Dear Sunny,
>
> What a dear heart you are. I understand what you mean because I had the privilege of meeting Dr. Norman Vincent Peale, Earl Nightingale, Bruce Barton and many others.

> I would like to reply to you with the words Bruce Barton used to me when I told him after his program in San Francisco that "In all of this audience today, I am the one who heard you. I have read all of your books."
>
> He took my hand and said, "Oh yes. I know you. You were the one I came for."
>
> You are the one I came for. Sunny."

Indeed I was! Life allows many teachers. Some of those teachers bring pain, some of those teachers bring joy and some of those teachers like Dottie Walters bring inspiration that touches and molds your spirit for a lifetime.

Since that time, I have gone on to believe in myself and to do as Dottie did, sharing my story with others in hopes of making a difference in someone's life, the way she made a difference in mine, so that they too could benefit from the wisdom and experience of an extraordinary and inspirational lady, Dottie Walters.

—SUNNY BOSSENMAIER · SUNGLOW87@HOTMAIL.COM · 970.565.3117 · LIFE COACH — CONDUCTING WORKSHOPS AND SEMINARS THAT HELP PEOPLE FIND THEIR INSPIRATION IN LIFE, AND DEVELOP THE TOOLS NEEDED TO ACCOMPLISH THEIR DREAMS · 631 EAST 3RD STREET, CORTEZ, COLORADO · 81321

Tom Marcoux:

Dottie lives on in my heart and in my books. She was my first mentor in the speaking industry. I learned from Dottie the spirit of service that the great speakers embody. I had the privilege to be coached by Dottie in-person a number of times and to interview her for my books, too. When I was with Dottie, she infused me with the confidence that I could do just about anything — that I could rise from where I was, and serve and live abundantly.

"Knowing what you know now, what would you have done differently?" I asked Dottie for my book, *Be Heard And Be Trusted When It Absolutely Counts: How You Can Use Secrets of the Greatest Communicators to Get What You Want.*

Dottie replied, "I would have believed in myself and not been so frightened." She told me about her childhood in a family with domestic violence. Her father's last comment before he made a final departure was, "She's not worth going to college." Dottie told me that his comment was like "knocking a kid down the stairs." Her self-esteem was crushed.

But her mother encouraged Dottie's reading and took her to the public library. There, Dottie discovered private coaches as she read the biographies of Albert Einstein, Joan of Arc, Amelia Earhart, Benjamin Franklin and others. These individuals showed her the way. Dottie emphasized that Einstein seemed to be saying, "Dottie, stop focusing on the problem and start concentrating on solutions."

One time, as Dottie was relaying this story to an audience, a woman said, "Who do you think you are? He didn't write that for you!" And Dottie responded, "Didn't he write it for all of us who needed him?" Dottie emphasized that on the day she really understood Einstein's comment about "solutions", she was alone with a book. The truth is that Dottie did rise to believe in herself and she brought thousands of people upwards with her.

Dottie opened a whole new world for me. Her inspiration led me to expand my journey from motion picture director to a communicator — and to add to my life by authoring twelve books, speaking in various cities across the United States — and being a faculty instructor to graduate students and a guest instructor at Stanford University. Dottie is with me every time I step in front of my audiences, whether they are members of the public or university students.

—TOM MARCOUX · WWW.TOMSUPERCOACH.COM · 415 643-0763 · AMERICA'S COMMUNICATION COACH "THE TIME-LEVERAGE DETECTIVE" AUTHOR OF *NOTHING CAN STOP YOU THIS YEAR!: HOW TO UNLEASH YOUR HIDDEN POWER TO PERSUADE WELL, GET MORE DONE, GAIN SUDDEN PROFITS AND FEEL GREAT!*

Jo Condrill

One of my favorite memories of Dottie is how radiant she was when we hosted a dinner for her in a restaurant on the banks of the Potomac River during one of her visits to Washington, DC. Bennie Bough, Ph.D, Art Jackson, and I were thrilled that she took time to be with us.

I am very grateful for having known Dottie. May God cradle her in His loving arms.

—JO CONDRILL, M.S. · WWW.GOALMINDS.COM · CONDRILL@GOALMINDS.COM

Brian Marinelli:

I deem myself to be enormously lucky that during the last few years of Dottie's life I got to know her as well as I did. She was not only my mentor but someone who I also considered a friend.

Dottie helped me numerous times during the first couple of years of my speaking business as I experienced growing pains.

A time I remember vividly took place after a *Speak and Grow Rich* seminar in Tampa.

Just a few days before I had presented my seminar *Unleash Your Winning Personality* to a group who were absolutely terrible. In fact, people actually asked for their money back right in the middle of the speech. I have no doubt that if the audience had things to throw at me, I would have been driven off the stage by a hail of missiles. I died a death on the platform that evening that professional speakers' nightmares are made of.

To me, Dottie always appeared to be an invincible figure in the speaking industry. She was so giving with her time and energy in sharing her wisdom with young professional speakers like myself.

I was devastated. With my confidence shattered, I was thinking of throwing in the towel and just accepting that my dream of being a professional speaker was just that . . . a dream, nothing more.

After the *Speak and Grow Rich* seminar was over, Dottie asked me how my speaking career was going. When I confessed that I was considering calling it quits, she wanted to know why.

Dottie listened attentively as I related my story of the previous night's events and how my seminar had imploded. Then with indisputable empathy, sincerity and compassion Dottie calmed my fears and re-energized the commitment to my dream.

The last thing Dottie said to me at the end of our conversation that night was: "Brian, this one bad experience is just a tiny blip on the radar screen of the great things you will accomplish in your speaking career." I will never forget that.

The stardust Dottie sparkled upon us ensures that her legacy and presence will never truly be gone. It will live on in our hearts and our minds forever.

—BRIAN J. MARINELLI · "THE CHARISMA COACH" · 813.975.8462 · BRIAN@BRIANMARINELLI.COM · WWW.BRIANMARINELLI.COM

Norma T. Hollis:

Dottie especially touched my heart and the hearts of everyone at Speakers Etcetera. She was my mentor and friend, and a true believer in diversity. Dottie was instrumental in helping me get my start in the speaking industry. I'm proud to be known as the "Dottie Walters of The 'Hood."

—NORMA T. HOLLIS · NORMA@SPEAKERS ETCETERA TEAM · COMMUNICATION EXPERTSSPEAKERS, · TRAINERS, COACHES, CONSULTANTS · VOICE 310.671.7136 · FAX 310.677.7981

Bob Bly:

Dottie was a friend and inspiration in many ways, but the single thing that stands out above all else was the story of how she got started: pushing her first two babies in a stroller, going door to door to sell space in her shopper's column.

In those days, women entrepreneurs and salespeople were rare, and she was attempting against all odds to be both. She was trying to sell small ads in a local newspaper which the paper did not hire her to do. Instead, she talked the owner/publisher into allowing her to pay for the space at wholesale rates after she had sold enough ads to local retailers to make a small profit.

And amazingly, because she was driven to and she HAD to, she made it work. The shopper's column was the first of Dottie's many successful ventures which later included a successful speaker's bureau and of course a magazine, *Sharing Ideas.*

What this incident taught me was that we have no excuse for not pursuing our goals, dreams, or ambitions. If an unemployed housewife could convince strangers to buy what she was selling, then there is no reason why I, you, or anyone else, can't do the same.

She taught me that it doesn't matter whether you were without the advantages you perceive others as having. Anyone can succeed if they are smart enough, or if they deliver a product or service with enough value, and if they work hard and persist.

——BOB BLY, COPYWRITER · WWW.BLY.COM/REPORTS

Stephanie Chandler:

FIVE THINGS I LEARNED FROM DOTTIE WALTERS

The numbered items are Dottie's words, not mine.

1. Never give up, help is at hand!
2. When you pick up the phone and call someone in need of help, they will never forget you.
3. We all have the ability to inspire others.
4. We all have the opportunity to achieve greatness and in order to do so, we must persevere.
5. We can work hard and make lots of money, but what really matters most is making a difference in the lives of others.

HOW I BECAME A FAN

It happened when I read *Speak and Grow Rich.* I devoured her book over just a few days during a hot Sacramento summer several years ago. I marked up my copy feverishly with a highlighter and sticky notes.

Fast forward to the summer of 2005. I was writing my second book, *From Entrepreneur To Infopreneur: Make Money with Books, eBooks and Information Products*. Dottie was on a short list of people I wanted to interview for the book so I sent her an e-mail requesting her participation. At that point, I didn't even have a publisher yet I got a contract with John Wiley & Sons months later. To my great surprise and delight, Dottie picked up the phone and called me that very same day.

She had no idea who I was, nor did she care that I didn't have a publisher. Instead she assured me that a publisher was on the horizon. Dottie exuded warmth and enthusiasm. We talked for over an hour and she shared some of her wonderful personal stories with me. She talked about how she ventured out with holes in her shoes, pushing a stroller with a ragged wheel, and convinced a local newspaper to let her write a shopper's column.

Later she met Dr. Norman Vincent Peale, the author of one of her favorite books: *The Power Of Positive Thinking*. She told him about her column and a few days later, he called her and asked if he could interview her for Guideposts. Shortly after that, he helped her sell her first book to Prentice Hall!

Incidentally, she shared an article about her life's journey that is archived on my website: www.businessinfoguide.com/article-dottie.htm

Ultimately, Dottie gave me a wonderful interview for my book and she sent me this e-mail following our interview:

> *Stephanie, I am so proud to be included in your new book. Congratulations on a wonderful achievement.*
>
> *Your Friend, Dottie Walters*

I had planned to attend one of the weekend seminars that Dottie offered in her home back in 2005, but I was dealing with a difficult pregnancy and decided to put it off. Now I am so sorry that I waited and missed the opportunity.

Even after her passing, Dottie's inspiration continued. I wrote about her in my blog and newsletter and received an e-mail from an author named David Evans. He told me that he too was touched by Dottie and had recently met her at a conference. He gave her a copy of his book, *Does God Speak Through Cats?* To his surprise, he received a call from her a short time later. Dottie reported that she loved his book and wanted to give him some promotion tips!

David and I became fast friends through e-mail. Compelled by his book's title, I also read and fell in love with it. I am convinced that Dottie's magic lives on in some powerful ways. She never hesitated to reach out and make a difference and managed to connect two authors who wouldn't have met without her.

Dottie Walters understood the art of "Paying it Forward." She touched people wherever she went and did so without asking for anything in return. It's little wonder why her fans are so devoted to her — she changed our lives. It is rare to encounter anyone with such talent and enthusiasm who is also willing to share. Dottie encapsulated this with her magazine, *Sharing Ideas*, to which I remain a devoted subscriber.

As a business owner and a writer, I often wonder if I'm making a difference in the world — something I believe we should all strive to achieve. Dottie will always serve as a reminder that I can make a difference and touch people's lives — and that with fierce determination, anything is possible.

—STEPHANIE CHANDLER · WWW.BUSINESSINFOGUIDE.COM · A SMALL BUSINESS EXPERT, STEPHANIE CHANDLER IS THE AUTHOR OF *THE BUSINESS STARTUP CHECKLIST AND PLANNING GUIDE: SEIZE YOUR ENTREPRENEURIAL DREAMS! 2006* AND *FROM ENTREPRENEUR TO INFOPRENEUR: MAKE MONEY WITH BOOKS, E-BOOKS AND INFORMATION PRODUCTS 2005.* SHE IS ALSO THE FOUNDER OF BUSINESSINFOGUIDE.COM, A DIRECTORY OF RESOURCES FOR ENTREPRENEURS AND PROPUBLISHINGSERVICES.COM

Ross Mackay:

In 1991, I had just been released from an executive sales position which had taken me around the world for over six years, thus rendering ineffective most of my earlier contacts in my industry. I decided to start my own business and use the training skills I had developed during that period. However, I had no idea where to begin.

Happily, I was guided to *Speak And Grow Rich*, where I received the recommendation that if I was serious about building a business in speaking or training, I should join both NSA and Toastmasters. I took Dottie at her word, and it was one of the smartest moves I ever made in my life. The combination of the different strengths of these organizations, together with the other advice I received from that book, catapulted my business into profitability by the end of the first year, where it has stayed and grown. I had the privilege of meeting Dottie a number of times since then, and was able to thank her personally, and every time we met, she was interested, encouraging and always taught me something new about the business of professional speaking. She was an important element in my being able to start my career and I will always be grateful to her for that as well as for the many ways she furthered our industry.

—ROSS MACKAY · AUTHOR, SPEAKER, CONSULTANT — HELPING EXECUTIVES ENHANCE THEIR EFFECTIVENESS · 905.726.9587 · WWW.ROSSMACKAY.COM

Anita Paul Johnston:

When I joined NSA after having presented about 35 of my own workshops, someone suggested that I attend Dottie's two-day training at her home. This is going back to 1996. This was the most enlightening, educational, and fun training. There was tremendous content, and Dottie gave so much of herself in her very caring way. I implemented many of her teachings which I know vastly contributed to my success as a trainer. Now 14 years in the business. I am also honored to be receiving my CSP this year. I have a special warm spot in my heart for our dear Dottie.

—ANITA PAUL JOHNSTON, PRESIDENT, ANITA PAUL INTERNATIONAL, • REALTIME MASTERY SEMINARS AND WORKSHOPS • ANITA@ANITAPAUL.COM • WWW.ANITAPAUL.COM • 702.240.8455

Andrew John Heath:

I had the pleasure of meeting Dottie at MVH's Mega Speaking Seminar in 2003 and 2004. Being new in the industry, I was amazed at how humble and sweet a superstar of the speaking world could be. Her love of dragons taught me that the crystal ball in the dragon's hand is the field of potentiality. I think of this often.

—ANDREW JOHN HEATH • AHEATH@HYDROGENCENTRAL.COM

Ana Tikhomiroff:

I met Dottie in 2002. I went to California to learn more about the speaking business and then, maybe, open my own company in Brazil. At the time, I didn't know much about the speakers' bureau concept. I was introduced to Dottie by Susan Levin, from Speaker Services. I remember driving all the way to Dottie's home in Glendora, worried about the meeting. I mean, I didn't know what exactly I wanted or what to expect from Dottie, but I didn't want to miss the opportunity of talking to her.

Dottie was very friendly from the moment I got there. She introduced me to everyone, even her dog, and showed me around. We talked for a few minutes and she took me to where she had all those videos from speakers, and folders, and tapes, and she showed me many things, she gave me tips on what to look for in a speaker: who had a good demo video and those who didn't. It was quite a lecture. She was so happy about my idea to open my own company. I remember Dottie even helped me with my company name. She told me the name should be meaningful, and that people had to look at the name and understand immediately what it was all about. I took her advice and that's why I named my company Palestrarte something like the art of Speaking.

I spent just three hours with Dottie, but I could have spent the whole day there; it was quite an experience talking to her, but we never stopped being in touch. She was always sending me emails inquiring about my business, saying she knew I would do a great job and would succeed. I also became a member of IASB because of her. She played a very important role in my decision to open a speakers' bureau in Brazil, and I'm really glad I had the opportunity of meeting her.

Dottie has also published two articles I wrote about Palestrarte in *Sharing Ideas* Magazine.

—ANA TIKHOMIROFF, DIRETORA, PALESTRARTE - A ARTE DA COMUNICAÇÃO • WWW.PALESTRARTE.COM.BR • 5511 5543-2775/ 5096-3222 (TEL/FAX) • AL. DOS MARACATINS, 992 CJ 41 A • INDIANÓPOLIS – 04089-001 • SÃO PAULO, SP • SKYPE - AEMBT28 • MSN - AET22@HOTMAIL.COM

A VIDA NÃO É MEDIDA PELO NÚMERO DE RESPIRAÇÕES QUE DAMOS, MAS SIM PELOS MOMENTOS QUE NOS FAZEM PRENDER A RESPIRAÇÃO! PALESTRARTE, BASED IN SÃO PAULO, BRAZIL, IS ONE OF THE MOST IMPORTANT SPEAKER'S BUREAUS IN LATIN AMÉRICA. THEY WORK WITH SPEAKERS ALL OVER THE WORLD.

Michael Levy:

Dottie Walters was a lady who knew her own mind. She possessed the determination, fortitude and courage to go out and get what she desired. In doing so, she helped many people to obtain their dreams and realize their aspirations. She was born a star and died a star. Her light shines on!

—MICHAEL LEVY • PROFESSIONAL OPTIMIST • WWW.POINTOFLIFE.COM

Sherry Knight:

In the mid 1980's I met Dottie for the first time at an NSA Conference. Smiling, affectionate and always laughing, Dottie enjoyed seeing others succeed. She took the time to talk to a novice speaker as if I was someone who really mattered, That's class!

—SHERRY KNIGHT, PRESIDENT, DIMENSION 11 LTD. • 2301-15TH AVENUE REGINA, SK S4P 1A3, CANADA • PHONES: 306.586.2315 • 800.303.2315 • SHERRY@DIMENSION11.COM • WWW.DIMENSION11.COM

David Evans:

While attending a meeting of Book Publicists of Southern California, I met Dottie about three months before she died.

A friend introduced me and I had a nice brief chat with her. She asked what I was involved in, and I showed her a book I had recently written and published titled, *Does GOD Ever Speak through CATS?*

She seemed interested, so I gave her a copy. Shortly after that the program started and I didn't see her again.

To my surprise, a couple of weeks later she called on the telephone, full of enthusiasm. She had read my book and wanted to suggest a number of ways she thought I could promote it. So for the next half hour or so she regaled me with one terrific idea after another. I was amazed by her generosity of spirit. Along the way she told me her life story. She also said she thought I should read the book that had changed her life: *The Power of Positive Thinking* by Norman Vincent Peale. I intended to buy it right away — but didn't.

Several weeks passed before I found myself in a bookstore buying something else and remembered Dottie's recommendation. So I picked up a copy of the Peale book. Two days later I heard that Dottie had died.

The whole experience really moved me. I feel a very special connection with Dottie because of what passed between us. I am also reading the Peale book! I didn't know Dottie very long or very well, but she really affected me.

—DAVID EVANS · DAVID@DAVIDEVANSCOMMUNICATIONS.COM

Cynthia Brian:

THE CAN-DO WOMAN REMEMBERS DOTTIE WALTERS

In 1999, I was producing and hosting, Starstyle®-Be the Star You Are!, broadcast from a radio station in downtown San Francisco. Our schedule was crammed with illustrious guests: Deepak Chopra, Jack Canfield, David Bach, Elizabeth-Kubler Ross, Wayne Dyer — and Dottie Walters.

Soft-spoken yet determined, Dottie was eager to share the information from her revised edition of *Speak and Grow Rich*. She believed in solutions, not problems.

Her mantra was "Yes, I can!" When her family was faced with financial disaster, Dottie rose to the challenge and began her own advertising business. She literally talked her way to the top becoming a master in public speaking, customer service, President of the Walters International Speakers Bureau and publisher of *Sharing Ideas* magazine.

What impressed me most about Dottie was her love of reading, especially biographies. She referred to the authors of her favorite books as "my friends". She felt that the books were written specifically for her.

"If they didn't write the book for me to read, who did they write it for?" was her comment when I asked her about her personal literary guides. Dottie loved the library and knew the names of her local librarians. When I was founding the charity, Be the Star You Are!, a non-profit that empowers women, families, and youth-at-risk through improved literacy and positive media, I thought about how Dottie educated herself by reading as much as possible. Books were her constant companions, helping her reach for the stars and landing on them. Following her example, my mission became to donate books to those who could not afford them, because everyone deserves to learn. I coined my motto, "To be a leader, you must be a reader." As of this writing, Be the Star You Are! has donated over $1.5 million worth of books to those in need of hope and inspiration. Everyone counts!

Dottie was speaking at the Learning Annex the week of our interview and she invited me to attend her presentation as her guest. Her grandson Michael graciously greeted the attendees and Dottie quickly won the hearts and minds of the enthusiastic crowd. Everyone walked out of that classroom armed with tools to be the next great speaker. She gave them the gift of "Yes, you can!"

Over the years, Dottie and I continued our friendship, chatting by phone from time to time. When I wrote my book, Be the Star You Are! Dottie enthusiastically penned an endorsement. We were one another's support squad, cheerleaders to success. I'd interview her on the radio, she'd profile me in her magazine. We would meet at conferences with embraces, smiles, and lofty conversation and I always felt motivated to reach ever higher after an encounter with the Dottie Dynamo.

Family was paramount in her life and she surrounded herself with loved ones. With her "can do" attitude, I found her to be always positive, funny, and outspoken. She envisioned herself as a leading lady while I pictured her as resolute as Hannibal who crossed the un-crossable Alps. If no road existed, she would build one! Dottie was unstoppable.

It was my great privilege and pleasure to have known Dottie Walters. I will always remember her as a pioneer on the planet planting powerful seeds of wisdom. The world is a better place because Dottie was here. Thank you Dottie for being the star you are and helping so many thousands of people sparkle and shine. We can do because of you!

——CYNTHIA BRIAN, STARSTYLE® PRODUCTIONS, LLC · CYNTHIA@STAR-STYLE.COM · PO BOX 422, MORAGA, CA 94556 · 925.377.STAR 7827 · WWW.STAR-STYLE.COM · CHARITY: WWW.BETHESTARYOUARE.ORG

CYNTHIA BRIAN IS A POPULAR SPEAKER, DYNAMIC WRITER, LIFE COACH, AND SAVVY MEDIA PERSONALITY WHO APPEARS REGULARLY ON RADIO, TV, AND IN PRINT. SHE IS THE NEW YORK TIMES BEST SELLING AUTHOR OF CHICKEN SOUP FOR THE GARDENER'S SOUL, AUTHOR OF BE THE STAR YOU ARE!, THE BUSINESS OF SHOW BUSINESS, AND MIRACLE MOMENTS®. SHE IS THE FOUNDER/EXECUTIVE DIRECTOR OF BE THE STAR YOU ARE! CHARITY TO IMPROVE LITERACY AND POSITIVE MEDIA. HER UPBEAT RADIO PROGRAM HAS BEEN BROADCASTING SINCE 1998 AND CAN BE HEARD ON WORLD TALK RADIO. CYNTHIA IS WRITING A NEW BOOK BASED ON THE THOUSANDS OF INTERVIEWS SHE HAS DONE WITH THE LUMINARIES OF OUR TIME, "GABBING WITH GURUS", AND DOTTIE WILL SHARE THE STAR LIGHT! CYNTHIA WELCOMES YOUR COMMENTS AND IS AVAILABLE AS A LECTURER AND COACH.

Wajid:

THE SHINING LIGHT OF INSPIRATION

Dottie Walters was truly an amazing human being. Many on this planet are born with a silver spoon in their mouth and do little to achieve a lasting legacy for mankind.

Others — through adversity, trials and tribulations — rise like Phoenixes from the fire of life's challenges. Carrying those who hold onto their inspirational feathers, they soar to heights and achievements their passengers could never have imagined they could reach.

I class Dottie as one of the latter.

Dottie was a fighter, a hard worker, and one who spoke from the heart with sincerity. A true lady if ever you saw her, always well-dressed, a wonderful host and charming personality who even took time to laugh at my silly jokes!

The day I met Dottie, I felt that she had always been my friend. She never judged a person based on their race, religion, creed or color but saw within each individual she consulted, a potential for greatness. She had the ability, with her coaching, to bring out powerful aspects of myself which I had no clue about. How did she do this?

By drawing on her own life experiences, Dottie taught those around her something which can never be replaced by taking a study course or reading books. Dottie Walters' legacy will live on to inspire, enrich and strengthen the lives of generations to come. The bright spark of inspiration called Dottie will not be easy to extinguish, in fact she will grow brighter and brighter for all to see.

Keep shining in the heavens for us dear Dottie, you are missed and loved, but will always continue to live and shine in our hearts and minds.

—WAJID WAJIDSPEAKS@MSN.COM · WWW.WAJIDLIVE.COM

WAJID IS A TEACHER, HEALER, COMEDIAN AND ACTOR WHO UPLIFTS AND ENTERTAINS AUDIENCES WORLDWIDE. HE EQUIPS HIS AUDIENCES INTERNATIONALLY WITH A FRAMEWORK FOR STRENGTHENING THEIR PERSONAL VISION BY SHARING THE SEVEN LESSONS HE LEARNED WHILE CLIMBING TO THE TOP OF MOUNT KILIMANJARO IN AFRICA.

Mo Bailey:

DOT'S OF WISDOM

I picked up the phone one day to "Hi Mo, this is Dottie Walters." Instead of replying to an email, she just called. She was so down-to-earth and special. I remember thinking that the way I felt must have been like those opening their doors to Ed McMahon with a Publisher's Clearing House check in hand. When I think about the lessons of Dottie, I think of them as "Dot's of Wisdom." This woman was incredibly generous with her candor, advice, contacts, and experience.

Her living example:

* Always be quick to compliment and give credit to others when due.
* Never, never — absolutely never — use foul language in a talk.

* Use stories to illustrate your point and be authentic, keep it real and reel them in . . . .

Dottie's integrity was the core of what I think most people felt about her: totally believable because she was who she exuded she was with no pretense. I don't think she thought out what she wanted people to think of her; she lived out who she was — a strong, independent, respectful and tenacious woman.

In the book, *The Solution at Hand; The Dottie Walters Story*, I read how Dottie felt that certain people came into her life at special moments for a reason. After speaking for years, semester after semester at Universities, it was Dottie who directed me on how to obtain sponsorship to allow me to spread my fervent passion and be compensated at a level I would not have received after giving it away. It worked! Dottie was the "solution at hand" and someone I will always cherish, who entered my world at a special moment.

I have vivid Dottie Walter memories. Dottie's reputation of expertise was embedded in my mind before I even met her. She was the lady who engineered the bridge for people to connect their visions to their reality. She is the example and mentor who exhibited the blueprints for all of us to follow.

At a time that Napoleon Hill has made such big resurgence in popularity, it is such testament that he asked Dottie to write a foreword for one of his books. I recall reading the testimonial Napoleon Hill wrote to Dottie in the mass email Michael MacFarlane sent informing the "Dottie world" of her passing.

A day I will always treasure is when Dottie invited me to introduce her at a seminar. She then gave me a book and personalized message for doing so. Later, she autographed two more books that I bought. I will hold dear the time she picked up the phone and called me. We spoke on the phone twice without a rush, and I always received eminently useful and sound direction. Although I was just one admirer in a constellation of her stardom, Dottie will always be a bright star to me. If you ever look up and see a cloud shaped like a megaphone, I think it will be Dottie speaking up a storm!

—MO BAILEY, FOUNDER OF WRITE4GOOD RESEARCH & COMMUNICATIONS, MO BAILEY & ASSOCIATES™ · 619.287.2822 · WE AWARD BUSINESSES, INDIVIDUALS AND SERVICES CAUGHT IN THE ACT OF EXCELLENCE . . . & PASS ON THEIR EXPERTISE TO YOU VIA THE FREE ACTS OF EXCELLENCE EZINE. SIGN UP TO RECEIVE TIPS, TOOLS & AWARD ANNOUNCEMENTS: WWW.WRITE4GOOD.COM

Eric De Groot:

Besides encouraging me to write an article about Dutch, Deutsch & Danish Cultural differences, Dottie also published my article in the Dec/Jan 1999 issue of *Sharing Ideas*. Earlier, when I phoned her as a new NSA member, she immediately started asking me questions about speaking fees, topics, programs etcetera and gave me advice that is still hanging on my wall ten years later. It's great to live with passion and be able to instill your passion into others, as Dottie did so superbly.

—ERIC DE GROOT, PRINCIPAL, GLOBAL EDUCATION MATTERS, A DIVISION OF E.E. INC · ERIC@GLOBALEDUCATIONMATTERS.COM · WWW.GLOBALEDUCATIONMATTERS.COM · VOICE 404.250.1709 · FAX 404.256.5437 · PO BOX 720400 · ATLANTA, GA 30358-0400

Dawna H. Jones:

It was 2003 and I was attending Mark Victor Hansen's Mega Publishing University in Los Angeles. As a budding author I was keen to learn about the industry and what made it work. One of the first people I met was Dottie. She was hard to miss. Dottie had a wonderful way of dressing that had everything to do with expressing her style and personality and nothing to do with worrying about whether she would fit in. This was the first hint that Dottie was no ordinary woman.

The second was the moment she opened her mouth. Warm and friendly, sincere and genuine, she felt differently from so many who were promoting their services largely because she cared about you and were curious about you and what you were trying to achieve. The focal point was not on how you could help Dottie succeed in her business; it was on how she could help you. This was different.

Make no mistake. Dottie was someone you could not underestimate. Her stories of how she started when times were tough revealed a shrewdness and quick wit that made her a force to be reckoned with. She had been on the full journey. She had plenty of self-respect which inspired me in particular, given that her generous nature was accompanied by a clear knowledge of her own boundaries on where she stood. Here was someone who could not be pushed around, yet she exuded heart and authenticity you don't find in front of a make-up counter. What you saw, was what you got.

The second time I met Dottie she was in Vancouver speaking to a small group of attendees. Though the group was small, she spoke to us as if the room was packed. Those not there missed out as Dottie always gave value to her audience.

Dottie was one of the very few high-profile speakers who answered her own phone, gave her number out, and who was not afraid to interact with her customers. There were no gatekeepers. No sharply honed mechanisms for ensuring that there was a wall between her and her customers. Rather she would listen intently to your situation, offer several alternative approaches, and always concluded by inviting you to share your experience and ideas with others through her magazine, *Sharing Ideas*.

It was at this seminar that she offered to give me a testimonial for my book. Grateful for the support, I contacted her. I sent her a copy; she sent me a testimonial. While this may seem small, it was monumental at a time when I was navigating totally uncertain waters in my life. The support from expected sources did not materialize. What was promised from others took a while to secure or did not come at all. Instead, it came from Dottie, freely given without expectation or conditional on purchasing her next program, or her next book.

People like Dottie seem rare to find, particularly in the speaking circle which is competitive, all for one, and a race to become high profile. Often it features more ego or self-centeredness than one would ever need at a time when collective endeavors are required to truly forge a future with hope. A gracious, generous, kind and yet strong and unassuming force, Dottie moved through the world achieving great things with little fanfare and quiet humility. I will always be grateful to her for lending a hand where the heart behind her action did as much or more as the act itself.

—DAWNA JONES, EVOLUTIONARY PROVOCATEUR · 866.605.0880 · DAWNA@FROMINSIGHTTOACTION.COM · WWW.FROMINSIGHTTOACTION.COM

DAWNA H. JONES HAS SPENT 25 YEARS HELPING COMPANIES AND THEIR EMPLOYEES EXPAND INSIGHT AND FORESIGHT TO ACHIEVE HIGHER LEVELS OF PERFORMANCE. COMMITTED TO DOING WHATEVER IT TAKES TO SPARK PROFOUND, LASTING CHANGE IN TEAMS, ORGANIZATIONS — OR WITHIN ONESELF –SHE CONSTANTLY PUSHES THE EDGE TO MERGE SCIENCE, METAPHYSICS, HUMAN AND PHYSICAL DYNAMICS TO OPTIMAL ADVANTAGE.

Carlos Gutierrez:

I met Dottie Walters at a class back in 1997 at Learning Exchange. I was an ESL student then and about to transfer to CSUS. I was recovering from back surgery, out of a job, with no opportunities, and I could only walk with difficulty.

I was looking for learning opportunities and possibilities. Because I was submerged in a wave if positive-and motivational speeches, due to my conditions, I got enrolled in Dottie's class with only one hope: to change my life. I wanted to learn how to become a public speaker, a writer, a good communicator.

I remember her very well. She was wearing a very elegant pink dress, and her presence was impressive. During her introduction she said, "You can do anything you can dream of . . . you can become a millionaire. Today, your life will change and will be different forever." I felt like a big angel had lifted me and that all my suffering and struggles were about to end.

During a break, I asked her for her advice. She said, "Stay in school, learn English, and get into motivational speaking, join Toastmasters and let your spirit fly. You can do it." I remember that I bought a set of tapes and books on how to be your own publisher, recorder, company and multiply your assets.

Today, seven years after my graduation, and ten years after I met her, I am starting to see the light. Thanks to what I have learned from her class and her personality, I can be in front of people in a big audience and be able to control my fear. Now my dreams seem to take form. I own my own Real Estate and Lending Company. I am writing an inspirational book, and a screenplay for a movie is being writing to inspire my community. I have been invited to speak at a Spanish TV News program as a finance expert, and a couple articles have been published about me. Without a doubt, Dottie transformed my life. She was and is still an **angel**. God bless her and have her in heaven.

—CARLOS GUTIERREZ, LOAN OFFICER/MANAGER, WORLD ONE HOME LOANS · 9381 E. STOCKTON BLVD., SUITE 216, ELK GROVE, CA 95624 · VOICE 916.873.1072 X 123 · FAX: 916.714.6960 · CELL: 916.271.1334 · TOLLFREE: 1.866.920.9645 · WWW.WORLD1ONLINE.COM · CGU@FRONTIERNET.NET

Dr. Jan Yager:

Just thinking of NSA San Diego and that Dottie won't be there this year makes me teary-eyed. She was one of the wonderful parts of attending a national conference. I could always count on Dottie to talk with me and to be enthused about my latest book project and all my speaking activities.

—JAN YAGER, PH.D. • WWW.DRJANYAGER.COM

SPEAKER/COACH/AUTHOR OF 25 BOOKS TRANSLATED INTO 17 LANGUAGES INCLUDING *CREATIVE TIME MANAGEMENT FOR THE NEW MILLENNIUM, WHEN FRIENDSHIP HURTS, AND EFFECTIVE BUSINESS AND NONFICTION WRITING*

Michael Podolinsky:

In 1982, I attended my first National Speakers Association convention in Chicago at the Westin Hotel. I was 26 and looked maybe 21. Shockingly, I had not one but *four* speakers look at me and say, "What gives you the *right* to be on the platform?" I would have been totally disheartened had it not been for Dottie Walters.

At the First Timers session, she approached me in her robust style, and asked me, "And what do you speak on?" I told her I spoke on martial arts philosophies as applied to sales and motivation. She told me it was a fascinating topic and was the first person to really make me feel welcome.

Then Dottie led me over to meet another speaker she thought I might have something in common with and introduced us. His name was David Goh from Malaysia. I guess Dottie surmised that the martial arts come from Asia and we were about the same age so we should meet. From that chance meeting, David and I became 'brothers' and he invited me in January of 1989 to speak in Malaysia. I now *live* in Asia and speak in Malaysia almost every month.

Dottie also got me started speaking in Africa through her bureau. This led to work in South Africa, Namibia, Botswana and Zimbabwe.

Based upon success in Africa, Dottie sent me to Mexico and Columbia. I had always wanted to travel the world and Walters' Wild Adventures division got me there so many times. Aside from the money I earned, the experiences provided a world of valuable insights and a global education.

Dottie also rekindled my passion for writing and actually saved my career. As a 15-year-old kid, I used to send articles to magazines and they would publish my writing and send me a check. Then a creative writing course in my university days ruined my writing as the professor who had never been published himself changed me from my usual conversational style to something more "profound." I started getting nothing but rejection slips and stopped writing.

Dottie told me just to write like I speak and encouraged me to be a contributor in one of her anthologies. I took her advice and being a co-author in *The Great Persuaders* really helped my speaking career and landed me a column in the local newspaper.

I went on to write chapters in two more of her Royal Publishing anthologies, *Marketing Masters* and *The Great Communicators*. Today I am a Pearson Prentice Hall author of 12 books and have sold well over 100,000 copies worldwide, all thanks to Dottie.

Dottie included quotations of me in her book, *Speak and Grow Rich!* and featured me many times in her *Sharing Ideas* newsletter. These efforts on her part to promote me not only furthered my career with clients but helped to raise the level of awareness of my work with my peers in the speaking community. She even ran a piece on how I met my bride and the love we share.

Dottie was an amazing woman and good friend. Dottie is still here in my heart today and in the hearts of the thousands she touched as her lasting legacy. Having Dottie in my life was a true blessing from God.

—MICHAEL PODOLINSKY · MIKE@MICHAELPODOLINSKY.COM

A 26-YEAR SPEAKING VETERAN NOW BASED IN SINGAPORE. MICHAEL SPECIALIZES IN "TAKING LEADERS TO THE NEXT LEVEL." HIS 700+ PAGE WEB SITE, WWW.MICHAELPODOLINSKY.COM IS LOADED WITH IDEAS, TIPS, TOOLS AND TECHNIQUES TO IMPROVE YOUR LIFE AND YOUR LEADERSHIP. MIKE@MICHAELPODOLINSKY.COM.

Phillipa Challis:

"Whatever it is that you decide to speak about from the platform, be sure that it is something that you are passionate about, that you love, and want the world to know about."

Back in 1998, I got those words from Dottie when I had been speaking for many years on several topics I liked and presented around Australia and overseas. My background in business and retail, rounded off by owning a public relations consultancy, meant I could cover many subjects when called upon to deliver a keynote or training session.

Her words fully impacted on me during 2002 after I added another feather to my cap by gaining certification as a laughter therapist, coach and teacher. After formal certification came the real validation: successfully delivering a presentation titled *Laugh Your Way to Better Business.* It left my audience laughing out loud, and saw them leaving the auditorium with smiles on their faces and happily talking with people they had never met before. They were giggling without my having to resort to jokes or humor. They were chuckling like children, and it was because I had introduced them to the newest mind/body activity sweeping the world — laughter programs.

Dottie told me to hone my skills on the platform, to listen and watch every speaker I ever heard at National Speakers Association and to learn from each one of them. She also said that to excel in my craft meant I would continually be learning new things so that when I stood before an audience I was giving them up-to-date information.

The most important message I gleaned from her was that the people in the audience were why I was there. I had to give them something to enjoy plus, whenever possible, something they could take away that would be of immediate benefit to them.

After five years of speaking on the subject of laughter and the way it can make life-changing differences, I have become passionate about spreading the 'happidemic' of laughter. Every presentation is a joy and I feel blessed that I have the opportunity to speak from the heart, and know in part it is because I took Dottie's advice and I speak about something I want to share. Dottie, wherever you are, I hope you are laughing lots.

——PHILLIPA CHALLIS, THE LAUGHTER LADY STRESS REDUCING AND ENERGY BOOSTING LAUGHTER PROGRAMS AND SEMINARS · PHILLIPA@LIVELIFELAUGHING.COM.AU · WWW.LIVELIFELAUGHING.COM.AU · VOICE: +61 3 5221 4266 · FAX: +61 5221 8628 · MOBILE: +61 418 521265

Dr. Bill Clawson:

DRAGONS AND PEARLS

Dottie welcomed us into her home with the grace and elegance of a movie star from the golden age of Hollywood. Yet, while we knew that we were in the presence of celebrity, we all felt very warmly welcomed. I was a member of a small group of budding professional speakers privileged to attend one of the weekend seminars Dottie Walters hosted in her lovely home in Glendora, California. She gently ushered us into her library and started our weekend off by telling us the story of dragons and pearls. She had a very large and varied collection of dragons adorning her library. She told us how dragons dove to the depths of the sea to bring up pearls of great wisdom to give to people who were ready to receive them. This tale was to be but one of many pearls that she shared with our group over that weekend nearly a decade ago.

Midway through this weekend, one of the members of our group gushed with a series of compliments for Dottie. While the sentiments expressed were what, I am certain, we all felt, the manner of the message was extreme and rather embarrassing. Dottie replied warmly and simply said, "Thank you."

She paused for a few seconds and then shared that most of us are taught to deflect compliments, that to accept praise is vain and immodest. "But I am telling you, don't do that! When you deflect a compliment, you are robbing someone of a precious gift they are trying to give you. Now, having said that, don't let it go to your head. There's always room for improvement; it's the biggest room in the house." With that, our group had a hearty laugh, only to realize moments later that Dottie had subtly brought yet another pearl up for our enrichment.

As our weekend together continued, Dottie brought home to each of us how there were at least a few things that we could do better and more uniquely than anyone else on earth. She enlightened us about the value of our words and our lessons learned, that people valued another person's experiences more when they had to invest in them. The lesson of throwing away our valuable pearls to creatures who couldn't benefit from them resonated in many of us from a Sunday school lesson long ago. We learned how essential it was that we record or write down lessons that we had mastered to share with others who were ready to learn.

Dottie went on with, "We all have the same number of hours in a day. We all have time to write at least one book, if not many."

She shared with us how the Universe of Thoughts and Ideas runs through our mind, much like a river, and when we are inspired, we should grab a pen and write it down. She disclosed her favorite location for inspiration was when she was next to running water, such as washing her hair.

She encouraged each of us to find and frequent our inspirational oasis. "I am amazed," she said, "by how many people are so selfish that they aren't willing to help prevent someone from having to learn only by experience. As we all know, experience is the most expensive school," she concluded, paraphrasing her favorite friend of the mind, Benjamin Franklin. Her lesson was as much as an exhortation: *Make the time to write.*

It seemed that only a few moments had passed and I was already flying back home from this outstanding weekend of learning from a master. As Dottie had affirmed, I was a good speaker; I also recalled and embraced her pearl about the biggest room in the house. It seemed as though the Universe had yet another pearl to add to the many I had already just collected: Perfection is a well planned accident; excellence, however, is a well planned journey. Although these are my words, I am most certain that Dottie must have said something similar. Indeed, Dottie had sent me and my colleagues off with a well designed journey, and well funded with many gifts of experience and wisdom. And my most cherished gift of all is that she called me friend.

—BILL CLAWSON, PH.D. PRESIDENT, QUEST FOR EXCELLENCE · WCLAWSON@PACBELL.NET · WWW.QUESTFOREXCELLENCE.NET · P. O. BOX 9050 · EUREKA, CA 95502 · VOICE 707.444.9200 · FAX 707.444.9300

Naomi Rhode, CSP, CPAE:

DOTTIE WALTERS:
A HUMAN BEING . . . . A HUMAN DOER

Meeting Dottie was an unforgettable experience, no doubt for every person she ever met! Her unique persona, her intense eye contact, her insatiable interest in your life journey and her potential place in that journey all came through instantly.

I first met Dottie when I keynoted at NSA in June 1977. She was the first person to greet me, and to express the challenge she felt women were having in the speaking profession at that time. She also had an immediate strategy for the potential role she felt I could play in women's inclusion and advancement in our profession.

One could either wrinkle one's brow at her forwardness, or immediately grasp that this was a woman, a human being who was determined to maximize every single moment and people intersection she was privileged to experience.

Once Dottie knew you, she never forgot you!

Her determined marketing spirit was inclusive . . . an arm spreading spirit of willingness to shout from her publications about your successes more loudly than about her own.

Dottie was a networker par excellence long before networking was a fad, or even a concept that many understood. She was a powerful agent for change toward a better world by helping multitudes of speakers sow the seeds of their expertise even on the planet's most remote fields in their quest for professional success.

There will never be a duplicate, or even a good imitator to this woman of influence and impact for the promotion and advancement of the Profession of Speaking. Dottie Walters will not be forgotten...a visionary strategist in our Profession.

—NAOMI RHODE · NRHODE@SMARTHEALTH.COM · SMARTHEALTH, 3400 E. MCDOWELL · PHOENIX, ARIZONA 85005 · VOICE 602.225.0595 X 214 602.225.0595 X 200 · FAX: 602.225.0599

IMMEDIATE PAST PRESIDENT, INTERNATIONAL FEDERATION FOR PROFESSIONAL SPEAKERS; 1997 CAVETT AWARD WINNER; 2003 LEGEND OF THE SPEAKING PROFESSION RECIPIENT; PAST PRESIDENT NATIONAL SPEAKERS ASSOCIATION; CO-FOUNDER OF SMARTPRACTICE

Dr. Reesa Woolf:

Watching Dottie work with people was a lesson in humility. Regardless of a person's experience, Dottie patiently explained her clever ideas with stories, analogies and examples. She left a big footprint on this earth.

—DR. REESA WOOLF · INFO@CONFIDENTSPEAKING.COM · 866.OK SPEAK · 866.657.7325

Terry Tillman:

I was recently at a memorial service where friends were sharing about the deceased person. One said, "She was my best friend." The next person said, "I thought I was her best friend." And the third person said the same thing, as did several more people after that.

Dottie was such a person. Even though our meetings were brief, and sometimes far between, I always felt her support like a friend. Dottie was a giver, and for me her biggest gift was encouragement. God blessed her, and blessed those of us who knew her.

—TERRY TILLMAN PRESIDENT, 22/7 COMPANY · TTILLMAN@227COMPANY.COM · WWW.227COMPANY.COM · 310.829.4777 · LEADERSHIP, TEAM-BUILDING SEMINARS / LARGE GROUP EXPERIENTIAL EDUCATION / PUBLIC SPEAKING

Paul Brosche:

Dottie's legacy of instilling ambition and compassion in everything we do will live on in all of us. She was a special woman. After meeting her in the late eighties at one of her weekend *Speak and Grow Rich Workshops* in Glendora, I knew I was in the presence of someone with great patience, passion and wonderful insight. I left that weekend, as I'm sure many did, focused and energized. Although I have not focused primarily on public speaking since that weekend, her sage advice has stayed with me through the years as I conducted workshops and advisory sessions for my clientele of small business owners and CEOs.

Over the years, I had the pleasure of sitting with Dottie in her Glendora office to talk about progress and new ideas for my practice, and I used every bit of her advice. Her first words were to raise my fees, and I did. I recall sending her a note some time ago, and remember that she responded immediately with a phone call and appreciation for thinking of her after seeing her at a local NSA conference in Palm Springs. Suffice to say, I know she truly cared.

I'm blessed to have had her in my life; she'll truly be missed, but not forgotten.

—PAUL BROSCHE · PAUL@PHBADVISORS.COM

Carolyn Cousins-Goldman:

I met Dottie Walters only once, but that one time made such a big impression on me. I would like to share my story, although I'm sure this same story has been told over and over again about this lovely lady.

Dottie was a guest speaker at a Speakers Bureau meeting I attended last year. At that meeting, she graciously offered a free 30 minute consultation to anyone in the room. My friend and I decided to call and make an appointment.

On July 11, 2006, we drove out to her home office in Glendora. When we arrived at 1:00 p.m., we were warmly greeted by this lovely lady named Dottie. (She wanted us to call her Dottie, not Mrs. Walters.) She offered us something to drink and we sat in her beautiful living room. We talked about professional speaking, and she answered our many questions. When she spoke with us, it was the same Dottie I had seen at the lectern a month before — the same down to earth, unaffected personality. As we all know, this is a lady who has known more than her fair share of famous people. My friend and I were not even close to being famous. Yet she treated us as if we were.

When we arrived, Dottie mentioned that she was working on a major project which had to go out that afternoon. Yet, she spent over two hours giving us the benefit of her vast knowledge and then showed us around her beautiful large home, taking us downstairs to see her offices.

On that day I'm sure Dottie was not feeling well as she died soon after. The legacy she left to me was the character she showed. Even though her schedule was tight, she treated us as if we were the most important people she knew and she was so gracious and generous. Dottie exhibited the signs of a truly great person. I thank her for the lesson I learned that day: People won't remember what you did in your life as much as how you made them feel. Dottie made us feel like royalty!

I'm not yet a professional speaker. However, I've been active in Toastmasters for three and a half years — more active than most members have the time to be. Before that I was a legal secretary for twenty-five-plus years. Currently, I dedicate my time to Toastmasters, my husband and four cats — to my husband's chagrin — in that order. But the cats don't seem to mind. We live in the San Fernando Valley section of Los Angeles, where I am enjoying a newly found freedom to pursue personal goals.

——CAROLYN COUSINS-GOLDMAN · 818.996.483 ·
KITTYKATZ@ADELPHIA.NET

Paul Talbot:

IT SEEMED LIKE YESTERDAY

In the late 1970s I heard about a great magazine for speakers called *Sharing Ideas.* It became my first introduction to the ever willing to share Dottie Walters. Young and new to Canada, I wanted so much to become a top speaker. I remember how the magazine opened doors and allowed me to hear and discover top professional speakers worldwide. People like Nido Quebein, Patricia Fripp, Kathy Alls, Carol Sapin Gold and Mark Victor Hansen. I credit *Sharing Ideas* with eventually being able to join the National Speakers Association.

In 1981 Dottie published *Positive Power People* to which I contributed a chapter titled *Stop Whining and Start Winning.* That marked a high point; I was on cloud nine, never suspecting that in 1993 to 1994 my world would fall apart. During this time I often called Dottie and she always responded with words of encouragement and wisdom. Because of her I continued to grow and learn. I remember during that downer time, Dottie said to me, (and to this day I can hear her voice) "Paul, there are no free lunches. You just keep on going and doing if that is what *you* believe!" And I did.

We met personally when she came to Vancouver for her workshop *Speak and Grow Rich* and as always, she was so gracious and willing to share her knowledge, skills and experiences with us all. Over the years we kept in touch with cards, letters and emails. She continued to encourage me which helped shape me into being the speaker and person I am today. Over the last thirteen years I have gained a reputation as a speaker on Clutter and have created my own Clutter series, published two books and one audio CD. It's all thanks to Dottie and her timely words of praise and encouragement.

Perhaps I am a late bloomer but I feel I have now made my mark. A big Thank-You goes to Dottie for believing and encouraging me to continue to follow my dreams, to not give up. I am so happy and thrilled that our paths crossed, and I know she is one of the brightest stars that will continue to shine on us all forever. With special blessing and thanks for a wonderful mentor and friend.

—PAUL TALBOT · WWW.DIALASPEAKER.COM · ADMIN@DIALAPEAKER.COM

Avon Drummond:

I spent a weekend at one of Dottie's workshops in Marietta, Georgia. She was inspiring and touched my heart. She really made an incredible impact on my life.

—AVON DRUMMOND · AVON54@BELLSOUTH.NET · 404.849.6247 · PRIMERICA FINANCIAL SERVICES, CHANGING THE DESTINY OF A GENERATION

Jacqueline Sidman, Ph.D:

I heard about Dottie Walters many times prior to actually meeting her. In fact, I was pretty intimidated by her reputation, and had been told: "You're not ready to meet her," by several people. "She's only for the 'seasoned' professional speakers." So, I didn't even try to contact her until several years later, after I had lost my home in Sherman Oaks in the Northridge earthquake, had relocated 'by chance' to Glendora, and had attended a marketing seminar in Las Vegas, where I saw her name listed as a resource in the back of the handout. I approached the seminar leader after the program and asked him if I should go to her training.

"If you have to sell bottle caps, GO!" he replied. Then I noticed her phone number was the same prefix as my new one.

"I think we're in the same neighborhood," I said. Sure enough, we were within walking distance!

I attended that first training, bought every product she had produced, and we were fast friends. Not only did she inspire my speaking, my education, my profession, and my heart, but she included me in her family. I was an earthquake victim, with few friends in that area, and she took me under her wing and made me feel welcome. This came at the turning point of my life. If I had not met Dottie and her wonderful family, I would not be where I am today. Her wisdom, guidance and kindness changed my life. I earned my Ph.D., have created a successful Institute and have made considerable contributions in my field. I was privileged to know her and will always cherish all I have learned from the great Dottie Walters. Most sincerely,

——JACQUELINE SIDMAN, PH.D. · THE SIDMAN INSTITUTE · 949.251.9550 · WWW.SIDMANSOLUTION.COM · 4199 CAMPUS DRIVE, SUITE 550 · IRVINE, CA · 92612

Alan Fairweather:

After spending a day with Dottie at her home in Glendora in 2005, I wrote a short book about my visit to California. Dottie serialized it in *Sharing Ideas*. Here's a section from the book in which I describe my day with Dottie:

"My original intention was to attend Dottie's two day *Speak and Grow Rich Seminar*. However, the seminar had to be postponed at short notice so Dottie suggested that she consult with me on a one-to-one basis. Although I'd have learned from the other participants on the seminar, I quickly realized that a one-to-one with Dottie would be much more beneficial. And so it turned out to be.

The day started at 8 a.m. when I was picked up for the short drive to the Walters' Ranch. It sits on a mountain called Ben Lomand. This is an immediate reminder for me of Ben Lomond, the highest mountain in central Scotland. It rises from the shores of Loch Lomond and is close to where I was born and brought up.

After breakfast, Dottie and I get down to work. She is totally focused on me and how I'll develop my career. The workbook for the *Speak and Grow Rich* seminar was used to highlight points I needed to concentrate on.

I receive so much information, ideas, tips, techniques and strategies for my success. I was also challenged by Dottie and made to realize what I had to do to make it happen.

By the end of the day my brain was bursting with information and I couldn't wait to get started on some new projects and finish the ongoing ones.

Dottie invited me back for supper in the early evening when I was pleased and privileged to meet her husband Bob and one of her daughters, Janine.

Dottie also took me for a tour of Glendora in her huge Cadillac. Coming from the UK, I'm not so used to such a big car. I had the impression of floating on the ocean in a huge bouncing bed; it made me smile.

I returned to my hotel that evening with very good feelings. I felt that Dottie had given me more than just the benefits of her knowledge and experience. She made me feel that she was interested in my success as a speaker. This had the effect of building my confidence and inspiring me to get on and achieve my goals. For this I thank her."

—ALAN FAIRWEATHER · WWW.THEMOTIVATIONDOCTOR.COM · THE MOTIVATION DOCTOR · 6 KEITH ROW, EDINBURGH EH4 3NL · SCOTLAND, UK

Freddie Ravel:

Dottie was my very first speaking coach and I will always cherish her loving spirit and lucid mind. Who could have asked for a more divine, gracious soul? I had the privilege to spend a summer weekend with her and a small group of fifteen to twenty other new speakers in 2002.

I had just become a father and was in the midst of fusing my career as a recording artist with my deepest spiritual yearnings, which are rooted in the notion that each human being carries a piece of the divine. My goal was, and continues to be, to utilize music as a tool to create profound communication and listening skills. I believe that this leads to the emotional essence of true listening-empathy. Now, has there ever been a more pure and empathetic persona than Dottie?

I'll never forget her graciously serving our group lunch and then going into the other room to take care of her husband who was bed ridden and fighting a variety of life threatening ailments.

She was very supportive and believed deeply in my work. She had asked me if I would perform a piece of music on my portable piano for her husband.

I set up the piano close to his bedside and performed "Water" an original, instrumental song. They both quietly listened. When I finished, Dottie and Robert shared with me that they felt that they were drifting peacefully together on the ocean. It was a precious moment for me because in that instant, I felt the resonance of the profound love that they shared for one another.

She loved the original title of my presentation, "Awaken the Music in You" but my larger goal was to work within the corporate arena to effect change on the highest level. A year later, when I came back with the new title, "Tune Up to Success", she loved it saying, "I love that tuning fork!"

Two years later, Dottie came to one of my shows at an outdoor venue in Pasadena. She smiled broadly throughout the whole show and we later celebrated by having dinner together with my wife and at the time, two-year-old daughter who Dottie loved to play peek-a-boo with.

Her whole concept of the "friends of the mind" made a very deep impression on the way I read, see, hear and share information. It's a brilliantly friendly and cosmic way of sharing the continuum of the flow of knowledge that we as students and teachers thrive on. Written with love and forever respect.

——FREDDIE RAVEL, FOUNDER, RAVELATION STUDIOS AND TUNE UP TO SUCCESS®, PREMIERE PRODUCTION, PIANO AND PERFORMANCE EVENTS I . . . "MUSIC TO INSPIRE, EMPOWER AND CELEBRATE." · FREDDIE@FREDDIERAVEL.COM · 818.386.5866 · WWW.FREDDIERAVEL.COM · WWW.TUNEUPTOSUCCESS.COM

Michael Modzelewski:

Like many speakers, when I was starting out and struggling to learn the business, one name I kept hearing as someone I must talk to was Dottie Walters. I called her office and she was kind enough to come to the phone. For the next hour, she patiently explained the first steps to successfully launch a speaking career. Her knowledge, fueled by a warm and caring enthusiasm, impressed me greatly. I applied every tip she gave, and also read her book, *Speak and Grow Rich,* highlighting and applying to my career just about every passage — and my bookings increased tenfold.

I talked with Dottie often and proudly appeared in her excellent speakers forum magazine, *Sharing Ideas.* After every phone call or article editing session, I came away with renewed passion and commitment to my work. Dottie Walters was a dynamo! You couldn't be in her presence — even if over the telephone — without feeling you were basking in the glow of a rare person who found her life's calling and was living her dream and destiny each and every moment of her life. Dottie was the living embodiment of the adage, "Make your passion your profession and you'll never work a day in your life."

As long as there is a speaker standing at a lectern before an audience — Dottie Walters will be there in spirit — continuing to guide and lift us all to new heights.

——MICHAEL MODZELEWSKI, TV HOST/AUTHOR/SPEAKER · ADVENTUREM@AOL.COM · WWW.PRIDE-NET.COM/ADVENTURES · VOICE 501.704.6879 · FAX 425.928.4961 · BOYNTON BEACH, FLORIDA

A FREQUENT CRUISE-SHIP NATURALIST AND LECTURER, MICHAEL IS THE AUTHOR OF: *INSIDE PASSAGE: LIVING WITH KILLER WHALES, BALD EAGLES, AND KWAKIUTL INDIANS AND ANGELES CREST, A MEMOIR*, AND HIS LATEST, *RIDING THE WIND*, NOW BEING DEVELOPED AS A MAJOR MOTION PICTURE.

John Aviantos:

Those of us that have been around for a number of years (I've been speaking since 1984) always looked to Dottie for guidance. She was *the* source for any challenge that a speaker could face, and she always came through — not only with the solution for the problem, but with additional advice to make the situation even better.

My respect for Dottie and her high level of professionalism is displayed in my purchasing over twenty copies of her great book, *Speak and Grow Rich*. In my opinion, this book is the bible for the speaking business. I was honored to give a copy to all up-and-coming speakers that had asked me for advice. They would always thank me many times over as all of their questions were answered by an expert and in great detail. They would relay to me that the book answered questions that they hadn't even thought of yet.

Best of all, Dottie was always caring and giving, even to new speakers who thought that this business was easy. She would gently guide them along, assisting with their development while constantly reminding them that it is not about them, but about the client and audience.

I am happy I expressed my appreciation to Dottie many times over the years. So often, people wait until it is too late to say how much they appreciated a person. I got to thank her over twenty times — every time I purchased a book from her — and on many other occasions for all her assistance over the years.

She made a huge difference in my successful speaking career. God Bless you Dottie

There's one in every arena. In golf, it is Tiger Woods; in basketball, it was Michael Jordon; and in the speaking business, Dottie Walters.

—JOHN AVIANANTOS, "COACH JOHN", "AUDIENCE EVALUATION DETERMINES HIS FEE" · OVER 2,000 PROGRAMS PRESENTED · WWW.COACHJOHN.COM · 480.949.8240

Elizabeth Kearney, Ph.D:

A WHISPER THROUGH THE VEIL

Once or twice in a lifetime, someone comes into your life and makes a major contribution to your world. Just such a person was my friend, Dottie Walters. I first met her in 1980 at a meeting for speakers, and as I sat and listened to her share wisdom with her audience, I was impressed that this woman was able to take complicated subject matter and translate it into guidelines that everyone in the room could understand and appreciate. That first meeting stands out in my mind but no more than other meetings over the years — meetings where she provided marketing tips, delivery suggestions, and leads to those who figuratively sat at her feet to learn.

Dottie always made people feel special, and I spoke to someone just after her death who told me that Dottie was the one person in her life who had made the greatest impact and whose advice had been truly golden. In other words, as she had always said she wanted to do, she had gleaned pearls from her experiences and shared those pearls with others.

It was from Dottie that I learned the importance of marketing approaches that were creative and client tailored, and it was from Dottie that I learned that the solutions to problems are always out there. But we need to look for them and recognize them when they appear. It was also from Dottie that I gained the greatest gift of all — the knowledge that is now being discovered by those who have read a book entitled, *The Secret.* She knew and helped us know that we are truly in charge of our destinies. Dottie's life was proof that it really doesn't matter where you start. What does matter is where you end up, and there is no question that Dottie ended up as one of the best-known speakers, most talented writers, and most creative marketers that the speaking industry has ever known. But, even more important, she ended up as one of the best-loved people in the worldwide speaking industry, and this fact has been recognized over and over again through thank you letters and awards.

Whatever she did, she did it with enthusiasm, creativity, style, and love — love for her family, for her friends, for her students, and for all of those who just happened to find their way to her "ranch" to gain the skills needed to make their own worlds richer indeed.

We'll all miss Dottie, but our personal worlds are far richer because God shared her with us, and I truly treasure all that I learned and all the kindnesses she gave me. I was lucky to have her in my world for over a quarter of a century. I can almost hear her giving us advice and sharing love like a whisper through the veil.

——ELIZABETH KEARNEY, PH.D., PRESIDENT, KEARNEY & ASSOCIATES: THE EXPERTS' ALLIANCE, A WBENC CERTIFIED COMPANY FOUNDED IN 1983 · P.O. BOX 1090 · SAN LEANDRO, CA 94577 · VOICE 510.614.8682 · FAX: 510.614.8683 · EIK1@EARTHLINK.NET · WWW.EKEARNEYALLIANCE.COM

Paul Lawrence Vann:

I met Dottie in May of 2002 at the *Think and Grow Rich Seminar* at First Class in Washington, DC. My life changed after that seminar, and then I visited Michael and Dottie at the NSA Convention in Orlando, Florida later that year.

Prior to attending the Magnificent Marketing Symposium in 2004, my speaking career was just getting revved up. After the symposium I decided to write my first book, *Living on Higher Ground,* and I did it in five months, thanks to Dottie's insight and guidance. By the way, I'm proud to say, Dottie was the first coach I ever hired.

What I'm saying is, were it not for Dottie Walters I would not be on the platform inspiring hope in my audiences. That's not all, I know Dottie supported our military troops because her husband was a veteran.

Next week I will be speaking for three consecutive days to the cadets at the United States Air Force Academy in support of their 14th Annual National Character and Leadership Symposium. I will let everyone know who Dottie Walters was; she meant that much to me. The speaking industry lost a Super Star, but heaven gained a Heavenly star.

—PAUL LAWRENCE VANN · PAUL@PAULLAWRENCEVANN.COM · LAUREL WREATH COMMUNICATIONS INC

Dr. Bette Daoust:

I first met Dottie through her books and tapes. Although this may seem like a strange place to meet someone, I really felt like I had the opportunity to meet with someone very special. I cherished every word she had put in print and also the words of wisdom on her audio programs.

Only a short while later I had another opportunity to meet Dottie. This time it was in person at a Learning Annex event. The biggest surprise was that my good friend Dr. Elizabeth Kearney was doing the introductions that evening. I knew that the woman giving the presentation was going to be one of my mentors and a person that would inspire me for the rest of my life.

Dottie had ways of telling stories that you could imagine being with her as she sold ads. I can still imagine the cardboard in her shoes as she schlepped from place to place. The bar that she described and the people she met not only influenced her life, but they have had a direct influence on mine as well.

It was only a week or two after meeting Dottie that I took a vacation and toured Southern California. I called Dottie and she invited myself and my husband to her home and office in Glendora. As if she had not already influenced me, she gave us (my husband and myself) a tour and introduced us to her crew. I had brought copies of two of my many books to show her and to my delight she offered to feature them in *Sharing Ideas*. I was most delighted.

As part of our meeting she coached me on many aspects of my budding speaking career. I still use those tactics today with great success. Dottie has been more than a coach, she was a friend, a colleague and much, much more. Dottie, we all love you and cherish your memory.

—DR. BETTE DAOUST, BLUEPRINTS FOR SUCCESS
BETTED@BLUEPRINTBOOKS.COM

Rolland E. Proulx:

I had the privilege of meeting Dottie when she was giving a one day workshop at the Learning Annex in Toronto, Canada a few years ago. I heard about the workshop through a friend of mine who urged me to attend because she felt this would somehow be important to me. I was left with the same feeling when I heard about the seminar, that this was a must event not to be missed. It was a challenge getting the funds to pay for the workshop at the time, yet come what may, I was determined not to let this opportunity pass. There are some people you meet in life that leave a formidable impression upon you. Even though the encounter may be brief you are left with an indelible feeling that is at once inspiring, uplifting and just plain energizing. Dottie Walters had that effect upon me.

Talk about déjà vu. When I first saw Dottie she seemed so familiar, a time of recognition, like I was re-connecting with an old friend. I knew at that moment that I was in for a remarkable time. There she stood at the front of a drab beige hotel meeting room radiating her stuff for all to share; we were in the presence of a giver. As the workshop progressed what struck me about her was her charm, confidence and common sense savvy.

Dottie gave a fabulous workshop. It seemed like there wasn't enough time, that somehow we were being cheated, denied the chance to spend more time with this wonderful woman.

The seminar was titled *Speak And Grow Rich.* What I learned that day on giving a presentation is invaluable. After all, I was learning from one of the best. Yet, oddly enough, what I got from Dottie's seminar touched me on an inner level that left me with a profound and far-reaching realization that changed the course of my life. Serendipity was at work. The magic phrase that rang out loud and clear for me was when Dottie was talking about choosing your field of expertise for your presentations. The question was asked by a seminar participant: "What should I speak about." Dottie's simple reply was that you speak about what you know; what else can you speak about with confidence and knowledge? She urged us to begin our search for a topic with who we are and to focus on what we know. Can it get any simpler. Talk about what you know . . . . Hello?

Meanwhile back at the ranch, my dream was to write and publish my work, yet the torturous issue I struggled with was, you guessed it, what do I write about? Dottie's magic phrase, speak about what you know, also became for me, write about what you know. This gave me the insight, the strength and courage to come out of the writing closet, to focus my energies and get on with the show.

The one day seminar with Dottie Walters was remarkable in that it left me totally inspired. I bought *Speak and Grow Rich.* Dottie autographed it for me: "To Rolland, our hero! All our best wishes!" It took five years to get my first book published. In my weak, doubt plagued moments, Dottie would come to mind and this gave me the strength to renew my efforts and move on.

I would like to share three quotes from my book, *The Electric Oracle Speaks, (Wisdom Now and Forever)* aphorisms for everyday living, in honor of Dottie Walters:

> *"The biggest limitations in life are the ones you set."*
>
> *"It's not what happens to you that matter. It's how you react to what is happening that is critical."*
>
> *"Impossible is a state of mind. Change it."*

I am forever grateful to Dottie. God speed, Dottie.

—ROLLAND E. PROULX · ARTIST\AUTHOR\DESIGNER · AUTHOR OF *THE ELECTRIC ORACLE SPEAKS* · WWW.ROLLANDPROULX.COM

Dell Dorenbosch:

Every generation there are those wonderful people, that wonderful few, who, like Dottie, inspire us. Then we go on and inspire others . . . the next generations; and the world is a better place. Things were so clear to her, just be kind, see good, be positive, speak well, educate yourself and help others — this is your work. That is how Dottie lived the printed text and spoken word from so many times and places.

I think of all the people around the world that have learned communication skills from this gracious, beautiful lady. I'm one of them and am so grateful. She invited me to write on Astrology — the Universal Language of the 21st Century — for *Sharing Ideas* Magazine in 2005, 2006 and 2007 after I did a chart consultation for her at her workshop in Atlanta. She loved what I did, said "please write for me." Instantly I was inspired!

She went to the next world on the day we celebrate love, that is what she embodied! I think she is getting the Angels ready to speak ... are you listening?

—DELL DORENBOSCH · 770.993.5885 · ASTROLOGERDELL@AOL.COM · AVAILABLE FOR PRIVATE CONSULTATION

Michael Wells:

I don't think it really matters that I never met Dottie Walters because the power and passion of her voice shot like a bullet through the telephone. I consider myself very lucky to have at least spoken with her. Dottie never knew me. Who was I? When I called her out of the blue, asking her advice on a speaking career, she eagerly shared her life experiences and wisdom and stayed on the phone with me for a long time. She talked to me as if she had known me forever. She cared and it clearly showed. She was the real deal. The spunk and upbeat tone of her voice would give this not-so-young newcomer all the reinforcement I needed.

If she could be so driven, so passionate, so in love with the speaking profession after all these years, then what stops me? At the end of the conversation, though she didn't say so, it was as if Dottie was saying to me, "I have given you my view, buy the magazine, and then go do it."

Faced with my struggle to realize certain dreams, I must confess that sometimes it's hard to remember Dottie's words, but then I stop myself, try to remember her voice and realize, as Dottie said, that be it speaking or any other dream, there is no other way. The baggage doesn't matter and you just gotta go do it — or not.

Thank you Dottie, thank you very much-for reminding me to keep going - no matter what. God bless you.

——MICHAEL WELLS, AUTHOR OF *SNAPSHOTS OF HEAVEN*, *FORTY FUNNY BUT PROFOUND REAL-LIFE STORIES ABOUT CHILDREN* · WWW.SNAPSHOTSOFHEAVEN.COM

Toni Henderson-Mayers:

My memory of Dottie Waters is so very dear to me. I was just starting out professionally as a speaker. I heard about the book, "*Speak and Grow Rich*". Many speakers referred to it as the, "Speaker's Bible." I couldn't wait to order it. I found Dottie Walters' website and quickly ordered the book. I finished the book in a day and a half. It would have been sooner, but I had to get some sleep. As soon as I finished it, I just had to tell Ms. Walters how much her book helped me.

I sent an email to the address provided and wrote how much the book opened my eyes and was putting my speaking career on the right track. Some days later, I was surprised by a call from Dottie Walters herself. She was so kind and obliging. I couldn't believe she took the time to call me. I wasn't a great name, I was just an average person making my way through the speaking industry. She took the time to call me and encourage me. She made herself available to answer any questions I had.

We built a rapport and I called on her from time to time for advice. She encouraged me to write a book and even offered to do the foreword of my first book. I was so excited. I wish I had finished my first book before she left us. I would be honored to have her included.

Dottie Walters will be missed. She was this industry's brightest and best!

—TONI HENDERSON-MAYERS · VOICE 877.511.0800 X 2 · FAX: 413.832.4279 · INFO@GOTONI.ORG

MOTIVATIONAL SPEAKER, AUTHOR, DECISION COACH AND ENTREPRENEUR. ALPHABETTHEATER.COM PROVIDES INFORMATION ON TONI'S SPEAKER AND COACHING SERVICES FOR THE PERFORMING ARTS; WWW.WISECOURTSHIP.COM SUPPLIES INFORMATION ON FINDING OR ATTRACTING A POTENTIAL SPOUSE AND FINDING A CAREER AND LIFE YOU WILL ABSOLUTELY LOVE! TONI WILL COACH YOU ALL THE WAY TO THE ALTAR.

What is service God?
Tis doing good to man.

—BENJAMIN FRANKLIN

Memories of Dottie

· Ande Rasmussen · Elizabeth Kearney, Ph.D.· Terri Marie · Bob Perks · Cheryl McLaughlin · Pauline DeLozier · RJ Jackson · Two Poems by Dottie: Supersale Magic and Plato's Magnetic Rings of Influence ·

In the personal example she always set, as well as in her magazine and books, Dottie gently encouraged others to emulate her devotion to sharing knowledge. In doing so, she touched the hearts and inspired the minds of thousands. A few of that multitude present their sentiments here.

March Forth!

March Forth!

When anything can happen

March Forth says it all.

If something does happen,

Get up, brush off, and March Forth,

Because we're all bound to fall.

—AndeRasmussen@aol.com

A Tapestry of Love In Memory of Dottie Walters

The greatest gift one can give another is the gift of love, and all of those who knew Dottie were enveloped by her love. A call for help was always answered, and her advice was laced with kindness and caring – caring words and heartfelt warmth. No wonder that all who had the privilege of knowing her will always remember her smile, her warmth, her sparkling eyes, and her beautiful face surrounded by a halo of lovely, red hair. All of this made this wonderful woman so special in the eyes of the world, and we are all so very lucky that she was part of our world. She will be sorely missed, but she left us all with a legacy too precious to ever forget — a legacy of caring and love coupled with the wisdom she shared so willingly to help us make our world a better place.

——ELIZABETH KEARNEY, PH.D., PRESIDENT, KEARNEY & ASSOCIATES: THE EXPERTS' ALLIANCE, A WBENC CERTIFIED COMPANY FOUNDED IN 1983 · P.O. BOX 1090 · SAN LEANDRO, CA 94577 · VOICE 510.614.8682 · FAX: 510.614.8683 · EIK1@EARTHLINK.NET · WWW.EKEARNEYALLIANCE.COM

In late autumn of 2006, a few months before Dottie died, I had been searching for a photo I had of her to include in the book I was coauthoring with her, *The Solution is at Hand*. I had taken the shot in her back yard, near her "Scottish Castle." In a true Scot fashion, Dottie had raised her left hand in a salute. I looked everywhere for that photo because I really wanted it in the book but it didn't show up until I thought of Dottie's salute. I had seen the salute on many photos I'd taken of her including the one in front of the Crystal Cathedral where she spoke to the Orange County Speakers Bureau less than a year earlier. All of a sudden I could imagine, Dottie standing in front of God right after getting her "divine orders." I could picture her smiling that bright smile of hers, telling God the words to this song as she came down to earth.

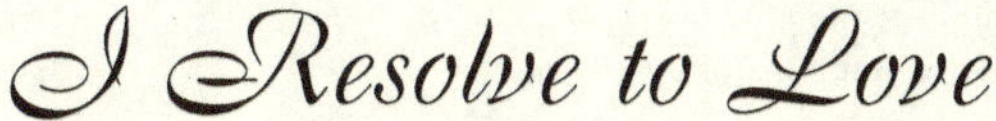

I resolve to love

I resolve to find a way

I resolve to care

Every minute of every day

I resolve to shine

I resolve to love them all

I will never give up

I will follow the angel's call

"Keep on going" I will say

To the ones who need courage

Help them find the gift in their heart

Yes, I'll do my part

"Don't give up" I will pray
When they're feeling discouraged
"You have come to do your part
When you live from the heart"

I resolve to give
To all those you send to me
I resolve to live
And share what you gave to me

Help them shine
Help them glow
Help them see what they're made of
Give me Ben and Albert too
To help see me through

I resolve to show
I resolve to carry on
I won't leave until
I know that my work is done

Then I'll shine, then I'll glow,
I'll remember their courage
When I return to you...above
Because I resolved to love

Always a Leader

The first time I met Dottie was at an NSA conference and she greeted me as if we had been friends forever. I watched her for a while. She was like that with everyone. Imagine for a moment how much our culture and national life would be enhanced if we all made each other feel that important.

Dottie was always ahead of us . . . always a leader.

I Wish You Enough!

(©) 2001 Bob Perks

I wish you enough sun to keep your attitude bright.

I wish you enough rain to appreciate the sun more.

I wish you enough happiness to keep your spirit alive.

I wish you enough pain so that the smallest joys in life appear much bigger.

I wish you enough gain to satisfy your wanting.

I wish you enough loss to appreciate all that you possess.

I wish you enough "Hello's" to get you through the final "Goodbye."

—BOB PERKS · BOBPERKS@MINDSPRING.COM · BOBPERKS.COM

For Dottie

Oh, Dottie,

You indefatigable curly headed

Woman, wife, mother, speaker, mentor, one heck of a saleswoman, and friend —

I swore you would live forever.

"Just DO something with it!" you'd say, and I jumped into action. "See their hands outstretched to you? They want what you have to share with them."

You fooled them, didn't you, Dottie?

You did it when you pushed your kids in the stroller, wearing cardboard-lined shoes, pounding the pavement for ads, and again on *What's My Line* with your grandmotherly smile.

You fooled them, Dottie, but not really.

You just did it a woman's way — fully.

You knew that in the midst of life's darkness,

That with Faith and Hope and a little Ben Franklin

Solutions would rise with the sunrise . . .

And they did.

You, my dear, left a long legacy

Of children, grandchildren and great grandchildren,

Of organizations you birthed to fill a need and grow careers,

Of courses that gave speakers the tools to succeed,

Of speakers who will share those tools filled with your memory as

They leave their own legacy.

You pulled many of us into the limelight,

Gave us a swift kick when needed and

Celebrated with us when we finally learned to own The Stage.

Thank you, Dottie, and Good-bye — but not really — because I see you smiling in the sky.

—Cheryl McLaughlin

Eternal Sleep

Dottie was an inspiration to me after we met because of her knowledge and enthusiasm, but also because we had shared so many similar life experiences. It was an era in which women were not encouraged to develop all of their potential. We both had been young mothers who said "Why Not?" and were encouraged by husbands to go past established boundaries. But it was not easy!

Dottie had me classified in a category she called "Pushing the Boundaries," but she was a first class example of how to do that, and in a gentle manner. Women everywhere benefited from her courage, stamina and wisdom. And so did men! She was a leader who carved a clear path for others to follow.

I recently came across a poem I wrote years ago. It was published by the National High School Poetry Association in 1957. Perhaps it is a fitting acknowledgement of a life extremely well done, so I send it with great love and respect for a remarkable pioneering woman.

Her eyelids blest with sleep.
Amidst the toil and want of life
To shelter she did creep.

Her trusting heart stretched out to God
Her soul found in His care,
Escaped from all unhappiness,
She finds no sorrow there.

Sleep on, loved one, sleep on 'til dawn.
The world will round thee keep,
Until, like thee, we each shall find
Our own eternal sleep.

Dottie left an indelible mark of optimism and hope. Now none of us can forget that "the solutions are always at hand."

——PAULINE DELOZIER · PDELOZIER@EARTHLINK.NET

A Friend Like Mine

Millions called her the greatest Motivational Speaker ever. Some called her Coach, Trainer and Consultant. I call her a woman of integrity, influence, and impact. Dottie not only made a difference in my life, she was the difference in my life. I believe that people come into your life for a reason and a season. The season for Dottie and I was short, nevertheless it was life-changing. The little time I knew Dottie forever changed my life and I am honored that she would call me friend!

I was first introduced to Dottie by the Internet as I searched high and low for someone seasoned in the speaking industry as a mentor. There were many great speakers to choose from, However, when I came across Dottie's information I was convinced that she was the one I needed to meet. I downloaded her information and cut out her picture and immediately placed it on my "wall of fame" and my "vision board". Unbeknownst to her, Dottie Walters became my mentor.

While on my quest to become a Professional Speaker I was determined to personally meet the one and only Dottie Walters. I remember the day I met Dottie Walters in Santa Monica, California at a *Speak and Grow Rich* Seminar. I was totally awestruck by her words of wisdom, her passion to see others succeed, and most of all her ability to keep her heart from wearing out by giving it away. When the seminar was over, I purchased several of her books, and got someone to take a few pictures of her and me. With the tightest grip ever, I held on to the two most important resources Dottie had given to everyone who attended the workshop: a sense of hope, and the words of her grandfather, "never give up."

Attending the *Speak and Grow Rich* Workshop increased my faith and set me firm on a path of purpose. But it was not enough. I knew that I had to meet Dottie personally. Following Dottie's advice being a visionary by seeing yourself where you want to be in life as well as what you want out of life, I began to see myself in Dottie's home, sitting at her feet while she shared her insight, experiences, and suggestions with me.

In March 2005 my vision became a reality. Dottie opened her home and most of all her heart to me, and I had the distinct pleasure of seeing the beautiful flowers that surrounded her home, meeting her "great friends of the mind" and sitting at her feet just as Mary sat at the feet of Jesus. Once again Dottie had given me a heart full of courage and hope. The time we spent together was indescribable. When it was time to leave, she gave me a tour of her home, walked me beyond her side door and to my car. She opened my car door, and said a prayer for me. From the moment I arrived at her home until now, Dottie had made a lasting impression. Then suddenly things turned. Dottie stuck her head in my window, grabbed my hand and said, "Thank your visiting me, my friend." For the first time as a professional speaker, I was speechless. Dottie Walters, a woman of integrity, influence and impact had just called me, RJ Jackson, "Friend!"

Dottie not only called me friend, she treated me like a friend. She would often call me, send me encouraging emails, and even send me letters in the mail. Once she sent me a poem, declaring that it reminded her of me.

A Friend Like Mine

Do you have a friend - Who says you're great
When you know you could have done better?
Have you got a friend who never replies
When you pour out your heart in a letter?

Or perhaps a friend who says it's your fault
When life levels you low with a blow-
There is one who has to "Pass it, for now."
When you needed them badly to "Show."

Or have you a friend like mine? Dear One –
That the name is all about,
Who opens my door and comes in with a grin,
When the whole world just went out!

Dottie once told me that I light up the room, but Dottie Walters was a woman of integrity, influence, and impact who lit up the world. I will miss her presence but she will forever be "my friend of the heart!"

——RJ JACKSON · 909. 820.6066 · WWW.THECOURAGEGIVER.COM

ALSO KNOWN AS THE COURAGE GIVER, RJ IS AN INTERNATIONAL CHRISTIAN SPEAKER, AUTHOR, CONSULTANT, RADIO PERSONALITY, AND BIBLICAL COUNSELOR WHOSE FOCUS IN LIFE IS "TO EMPOWER OTHERS TO RELEASE THEIR FEARS AND PROCEED WITH COURAGE."

And, lastly, two poems that Dottie wrote that express her philosophy succinctly:

Supersale Magic

Many will tell you
The "Secret of Sales."
They'll give you the "Why" and the "How."
But I believe there are
Four Magic Words
That will overcome, "No, not now!"

First you must listen,
Lean forward and smile.
Think just of your customer's need
Watch movements — and 'eye-talk':
Sharp focus your mind
For herein lies the seed.

Now ask gentle questions;
Be careful to care.
When they tell you problems and trouble.

Say, Oh, I am sorry . . ."

Then, "Here's what will work."

Do *this* and your profits will double!

Whenever a customer

Whispers a word,

Remember this answer, don't doubt it.

Lean forward and listen,

Lean forward and smile . . .

Four magic words,

"Tell me about it!"

Plato's Magnetic Rings of Influence

Mentors and Mentees are circles that meet!

Magnetic power that surges, complete.

Down through the ages, the Mentors reach out

To Mentees, the seekers, and touching, they shout:

"Pass on the power, don't let it stop here,

Give of your knowledge." [a mandate] "Now hear!

Search for your Mentee, and power you'll find;

When you are the Mentor, magnetic your mind."

A light through the years, the ideas flow:

Plato is smiling, his rings all aglow.

—DOTTIE WALTERS

Plato's Rings

This gift which you have . . . is not an art, but an inspiration: there is a divinity moving you, like that in the stone which Euripedes calls a magnet, but which is commonly known at the stone of Heraclea. For that stone not only attracts iron rings, but also imparts to them a similar power of attracting other rings, and sometimes you may see a number of pieces and rings suspended from one another so as to form a long chain; and all of them derive their power of suspension from the original stone. Now this is like the Muse, who first gives men inspiration herself and from these inspired persons a chain of other persons is suspended, who take the inspiration from them."

—PLATO ION. SEC 533.

This simile has come to be known as "Plato's rings."

The hard work and poverty of my childhood turned out to be my greatest asset in later years.
Nothing could ever seem too hard after that.

—SUE SANDERS, US OIL PRODUCER

Her father died when she was five. Sue married a hardscrabble farmer at fourteen. After suffering serious financial and emotional problems with him, she split from her husband at eighteen. Taking their two babies with her, Sanders went on to become a highly successful businesswoman.

What Speakers You Know Say About Dottie

· JACK CANFIELD · NAPOLEON HILL ·
EARL NIGHTINGALE ·

Dottie not only joined the top ranks of paid professional speakers, she led the charge to bring order and high ethics to this field that, as she entered it, was almost like the OK Corral in Tombstone, Arizona. She proved her worth by crashing through or ignoring all barriers. The reforms she urged in her soft voice and wonderfully reasonable manner were perfectly timed and badly needed — so they were quickly adopted.

Jack Canfield:

(Excerpted from his foreword to *The Solution is at Hand — Dottie Walters and Terri Marie.)*

> "I first met Dottie Walters at a National Speakers Association meeting over 20 years ago. I was immediately struck by her deep wisdom, her generous spirit, and her amazing breadth of knowledge about speaking and writing. I was just breaking into the world of professional paid speaking after years as a high school teacher and trainer of teachers. I eagerly signed up for Dottie's magazine for speakers, *Sharing Ideas*, and waited eagerly every month for its arrival so that I could learn more about how to take my message of self-esteem and self-empowerment to more and more people. I would read every article, underlining all of the books that were reviewed, and I read all the ads and ordered cassette tapes, manuals and anything else that I thought would help. I somehow knew I could trust Dottie and the people and resources she recommended and endorsed. I could just feel her sincere desire to help.
>
> Years later I moved to the Los Angeles area and actually got to visit Dottie in her home in Glendora. I was treated like an old friend visiting. My love

and respect for Dottie grew deeper. Over the years, Dottie and I have crossed paths many times. Her wonderful story *Failure? No! Just Temporary Setbacks* appears in our first *Chicken Soup for the Soul* book, which was translated into 47 languages and has sold more than ten million copies around the world. Later, like a boyhood dream come true, Dottie featured me on the cover of *Sharing Ideas* in 1992 and Mark Victor Hansen, my *Chicken Soup* co-author, and me again in 1995. Dottie and her daughter Lilly's book *Speak and Grow Rich* is like a bible among professional speakers, and I have told literally thousands of wannabe speakers to study that book if they want to be successful.

Dottie is more than a personal friend. She is an icon of success who shows you what possibilities in life might unfold for you, if you follow her example and *never give up*. Dottie's remarkable story and the stories of the people she has mentored would fill an entire *Chicken Soup for the Soul* book. . . ."

—JACK CANFIELD · CO-CREATOR OF THE *CHICKEN SOUP FOR THE SOUL* SERIES AND AUTHOR OF *THE SUCCESS PRINCIPLES*

Dottie Walters:

"When *Never Underestimate the Selling Power of a Woman* was first published, I appeared on many national television shows. Napoleon Hill, the author of *Think and Grow Rich* wrote to me:

> "Congratulations Dottie Walters. You've made the Big League in the world of authoring and selling. I have a copy of your new book and assure you it's a masterpiece.
>
> So glad my good friend and protégé Earl Nightingale has written the introduction to your book. Your appearance on *To Tell The Truth* was priceless.

Today, Mrs. Hill and I were watching television when *To Tell The Truth* came on. Of course I recognized you as I had seen your picture on the jacket of your book. Just to have a little fun I wagered a bet with Mrs. Hill that I could pick the right Dorothy Walters, and sure enough I did! Mrs. Hill hadn't seen your book up to that time but she wondered why I was so sure I had picked the right person until I slyly slipped your book into her hands.

Best wishes, Dorothy, and enduring affection. How does it feel to have blown to the world a handful of inspirational star dust?

Enthusiastically,

Napoleon Hill"

THE NAPOLEON HILL FOUNDATION · A NON-PROFIT EDUCATIONAL INSTITUTION DEDICATED TO MAKING THE WORLD A BETTER PLACE IN WHICH TO LIVE. · BOX 1721 · COLUMBIA, SOUTH CAROLINA

Excerpted from the foreword of *Never Underestimate the Selling Power of a Woman:*

Earl Nightingale's syndicated radio program Our Changing World provides a daily source of courage, incentive, faith, and peace of mind for several million listeners. His record, The Strangest Secret is the most popular talk record of all time and he is Chairman of a firm which produces broadcast and motivational material.

——DOTTIE WALTERS, 1986

"At last an intelligent, common sense, workable, money-making book for women!

"I have long said that every woman should have an interesting and rewarding line of business she can turn to, not just in the case of financial need, but as a means of keeping young, busy and active.

"Women have always been the world's best "salesmen." Any man who has ever been asked for a new coat knows that his arguments are in vain. Sooner or later, he will buy her the coat — and the handbag, hat and shoes to match.

"Long before Cleopatra "sold" Julius Caesar on appointing her Queen of Egypt and later convinced Mark Anthony to fight a war for her, women have been getting their way in the world.

"Now, here is a book, written by a woman who really knows what she's talking about, which can help any woman make her way in the world of selling — the world's most interesting and highest paid profession.

"Selling is communicating. Good selling is good communicating. Great selling is great communicating. This takes preparation, knowledge and planning. It means finding out how to get started, where and with what. . . ."

——EARL NIGHTINGALE

He was a young Marine corporal aboard the USS Arizona when it was destroyed by Japanese planes in their surprise attack on America's Pacific Battle Fleet as it lay at anchor in Pearl Harbor. Nearly twelve hundred men on the Arizona lost their lives. Miraculously, Earl Nightingale was among the few who survived.

Undertake something that is difficult; it will do you good.
Unless you try to do something beyond what you
have already mastered, you will never grow.

— Ronald E. Osborn

10

Family Recollections of Their Gifted Lady

· Dottie's Son, Michael Walters · Dottie's Daughter, Jeanine Walters · Dottie's Grandson, Michael MacFarlane · Dottie's Grandson, John King · Dottie's Daughter-in-Law, Mayleta Walters ·

Until the last few weeks of her life, Dottie usually answered the phone at *Sharing Ideas, The International Newsmagazine for Speakers, Meeting Planners, Agents, Bureaus, Trainers and Seminar Leaders.* Because she was so readily available, few of us gave much thought to how she managed that and still be highly productive in so many other ways. Great unflagging energy and the habit of putting in very long hours doing what she loved were the foundations of a lifetime of achievement. Those qualities were buttressed by a storybook romance with her husband that lasted her entire adult life, and by wonderfully affectionate relationships with her descendants.

Michael Walters:

I'm the first born and started working with my parents when I was eleven years old. In my lifetime I must have loaded and unloaded a hundred million pounds of Hospitality Hostess material in and out of our station wagon. I was in the Boy Scouts and ended up becoming an Eagle Scout.

It was understood early on that I was going to college. And, as the first in our family to go to college, of course I had to get a doctorate.

Dottie was a hands-on mom. I had a good childhood and have no complaints but it was different from being a child in other families. While being interviewed for the Linkletter TV Show, I was asked if I'd rather be out playing baseball with other kids than making plates in my father's print shop. I answered, "No. I wouldn't be paid to play baseball."

I was always goal oriented. I'm a self-motivated person, a lot like my mom. It was assumed that when I graduated from college I'd join the family business. However, by the time I was in college things were changing.

Everybody in town knew my parents. Dad had lots of friends and was President of the Chamber of Commerce and President of the Kiwanis twice. Loads of people knew and respected Mom. So between Mom and Dad I couldn't get away with anything, Every year Mom sent out Christmas cards with our pictures to merchants, clients, friends and employees, much to my embarrassment because my friends would see them. One year she sent out a picture of us exiting the Cornerstone Church in Glendora at Christmas time. This was not our regular church but it was chosen for the stairs and a lot of people called me on it.

As an adult, I looked forward to going to the house on New Year's Eve, which was also Mom's birthday. It was always a big party with the most fascinating cross section of people: politicians, clergymen, and businesspeople mingling with magicians, palm readers, taro readers, fortune tellers and psychics — a couple hundred guests or more,

Mom was somewhat one-dimensional with her focus on the business. She had little time for anything else, so we ate out a lot. To say Mom was cooking-challenged would be an extreme understatement. She didn't enjoy it. She used to tell us if we didn't get up in the morning, she would make breakfast!

When I was a kid I forgot to tell Mom that I needed to bring two dozen cookies to school. It was too late to have our maid bake them and I don't think Mom even knew how to bake cookies. So she bought something like Chips Ahoy packaged ones, slid them into the oven so they'd bake up uneven and look homemade. She told that story on herself. She had a solution for everything.

I cooked a little, Jeanine and Mom cooked some, but mostly we ate out. We had help with the house every day.

Mom used to send people to me, as I'm a public speaker too. One woman who contacted me wanted to consult with corporations about how their employees could be encouraged to lead a balanced life. I don't know of anyone who is achieving anything in life who lives a balanced life. I don't want my employees living balanced lives. Remember, I'm a lawyer. I work twelve to fourteen hours a day six days a week.

I don't understand this whole idea of balance. If you love your work then you don't work a day in your life. Mom loved her work, Dad loved his work. I love my work. No one in our family ever worked for wages. We didn't think in terms of having a job . . . we were businesspeople. There was no idea that work and family life were two different areas. We were more like the farming families a few generations back. I think our family was much more traditional in that respect than most.

Dad accompanied Mom on many speaking trips. I think he was the only person who could have been married to Mom. He was a Marine Master Sergeant in WWII, and was awarded the Bronze Star. He was a masculine cowboy who loved horses. As a kid, I owned a horse.

Someone told my dad, "Oh, you're married to Dottie Walters. I would never let my wife work."

Dad replied, "Well, you must never have met my wife!"

Dad invested in real estate and I was seventeen years old before I found out that weekends were not for the purpose of painting apartments. He was very hands-on in acquiring apartments, fixing them up, renting and reselling property. The first words of Spanish I learned were: "Where's the rent?"

When my mom's business was taking off, she had trouble finding a reliable printer. Dad left his job and set up a printing operation. Within two years he had the largest print shop in the county. He was very practical and good at implementing her ideas. He was active in the Hospitality Hostess business as well.

I helped in the print shop more than I worked in Mom's office while I was attending college. Because I worked through school I felt that getting excited about the next big game was silly. The work ethic I was exposed to was the overwhelming experience of my life. I love my work. My work is my hobby.

Dad gave me a '53 Chevrolet convertible, which was a cool car. We had a sailboat near our rental property in San Diego and I'd go sailing sometimes. Usually a sailing outing to San Diego involved painting an apartment.

My parents overwhelming philosophy of life was, "You can do it." They lived it every day of their lives. Not only that, but as kids we were *expected* to accomplish whatever needed doing.

Holidays were traditional family times. At Christmas we had a huge decorated tree. On the Fourth of July we all watched fireworks from our terrace and had a cook-out.

Every dinner out as a family featured discussions about business — always. When I was in college, I envied friends who had lawyers in their family. They were light-years ahead of me: I think it took me a year to figure that out.

I attended Cal Poly and then graduated from Cal-Western Law School in San Diego. I didn't work the first year of college but after that I managed my parents' apartments, had two or three other jobs and went to law school. I just didn't sleep. Now I have a beautiful wife and home and make a great living.

I remember watching one of Mom's interviews on TV. She was asked if she had been discriminated against when she was starting out since there were so few women in business at that time. She said she had been discriminated against many times. For instance she wasn't allowed to join the Chamber of Commerce when she first applied. But she got to know many of the members and pretty soon she was allowed in.

The interviewer said, "I'll bet you were called upon to make the coffee."

"Only once!" my mother replied.

I wrote a column in the 1980s in the local paper about a meeting with a group of women where one lady announced, "I'm President of the local Chamber." Another said, "I'm a homemaker and have four kids but I read a lot." Mom said, "I have my own business and my son is an Eagle Scout."

Mom never looked down on full-time homemakers. That wasn't her way.

A clergyman lost his lease and needed to find a temporary church right away. He came to Mom. She saw something he hadn't realized: he didn't need a brick or stucco building topped by a bell tower; he needed a place where his congregation could gather to worship. She called the owner of a drive-in movie and said, "You're not using your property on Sundays, would you rent it to a church for Sunday Services?" This was in Southern California, where it never rains in the summer.

It made great sense to my practical, solutions-oriented Mom. A drive-in would have plenty of parking; it had a sound system with speakers that connected to the cars; and it was deserted on Sunday mornings. But the pastor was uncomfortable with the drive-in church idea and questioned Mom about it.

Dottie said, “Are you kidding? Call the newspapers and radio. You have the first drive-in church!” He did. The drive-in It was a tremendous success, in part because of the huge amount of publicity this far-out idea generated.

The drive-in came to mind because families could bring their children there. This also sums up Mom’s willingness to help. With her innovative ideas, she put many people together. As often happened, others saw a crisis, Dottie saw an opportunity.

Bob Schuller, the pastor, went on to build the spectacular Crystal Cathedral that ranks high among the nation’s most awesome and inspiring structures glorifying God’s gifts to humankind. It has long been one of the greatest attractions in the Golden State.

I started conducting seminars on trusts because other attorneys were complaining about spending too much time in their office explaining them to clients. Now the twenty, two-hour workshops on wills and trusts that I conduct monthly draw the largest audiences of any similar workshops in California.

Jeanine Walters

I’ve been problem solving since I was a little girl. I learned that you should know what you’re going to do, then do it. Being a high school teacher now, I see many teenagers who have never been taught how to solve a problem.

As little kids, if my brother and I fought we were sent to our rooms to make a list of how we were not going to do that again. It was invaluable training because it got me out of some scraps, and allowed me to think things through.

Career-wise I had a problem with my parents for many years. They were unhappy that I was *only* a teacher. Not until late in Mom's life did she realize what an important job teaching is.

We were expected to work in the family business. My brother being an attorney and I being a teacher were on the *list* for a long while. We would help out at times and be considered part of the business even if we weren't there.

I did learn about business working with my mother and that fact makes me unique as a teacher. When you attend college, you don't necessarily understand management. It assists me in understanding budgeting, hiring, firing, and so on.

Dottie was so pleased that my oldest son, Michael, became part of the family business. She always wanted five kids so she felt that mine were hers. I had just happened to give birth to them. She helped Michael by teaching him the business and he just fell in love with the business and he really respected his grandmother.

Dottie helped my youngest son, John, to attend chef's school. John reminds me so much of my dad. He's a dedicated father . . . loves his kids and his family.

My father, Bob, was the perfect mate for my mother. He was the love of her life and she was the love of his. They worked as partners. A big lesson in my life was watching them work together. We would sit down at the dinner table and discuss a family problem. How each of us could help. From the time we were kids, we were all partners in the family. Mom and Dad were certainly partners for life. They respected each other.

Dad was asked if it bothered him that Dottie was so successful. He responded, "No. This is what she wants to do. Why would I not want her to be happy?" They both supported each other in every way. I did join Mom on some speaking engagements but mostly it was Dad. Then Michael took over. I did some consulting with speakers and assisted Dottie when she had seminars in her home. I prepared the food, greeted people, participated in seminars and did all the things she didn't have time for.

Part of my mother's appeal was that she genuinely cared about her clients and all the people she did business with. She loved journalism and from her experiences in high school, she started the Hospitality Hostess service. Her philosophy was that when we share our ideas and share with people, it doesn't mean we're not competing, but we're helping each other.

Recently, I traveled to Texas to accept the Lifetime Achievement Award from the International Association of Speakers Bureaus that Mom co-founded.

When I was very young I helped with collating and stuffing envelopes. Later on, I helped welcome new residents. Instead of giving me college tuition, Mom gave me a job. I worked in her office in San Diego. It made me appreciate my education even more by working for it.

The trouble-shooting in the business helped me out. Sometimes someone would quit or have other problems and I would need to take over their tasks or sometimes redo their work. The hardest thing I did happened one summer after I finished my Master's Degree. Mom wanted me to take the job of whoever was away from the office.

The toughest was being her secretary. The pace was so hectic that I could never catch up on anything. I followed her around with pen and pad creating or solving problems constantly. I wasn't a trained secretary, so I was glad to see her regular secretary return from vacation. By that time, I really appreciated all she took on. Bea Nelson was Mom's secretary for a very long time. She truly cared about my mother.

Mom and Dad took me and my brother to Mexico City and the Mayan ruins. So we would better understand the history, she brought along a book titled *The Discovery and Conquest of Mexico* by Diaz del Castillo. He was one of the conquistadors with Hernando Cortés. She read that book to us on the trip.

Mom liked nonfiction and read to us a lot as we grew up. If we were going someplace, she wanted us to have a deeper appreciation of the area. Once our entire family went on a cruise together, but mostly travel was arranged around her speaking engagements.

Fortunately, Dad was around; he was the nurturer. Because we helped with the family business, we got to be with our parents more than most children growing up. But as a teenager I was jealous of kids who got to work at the hamburger stand because I had to help at home with the business. Later something dawned on me. The kids who had to work at the hamburger stands were jealous, because I worked in my family's business. When we were young we had debit and credit books. Each week Dad would go over what jobs we worked on or completed and we were paid. When we did something we shouldn't have done, that was deducted.

Dad had this thing, since he and Mom had started dating, that no matter where they were in the world, he would always remember Mom on Valentine's Day. Whether he was in the South Pacific as a Marine, or even after he fell ill, he'd tell us kids what to get and send us out to buy it. He had wonderful taste and gave her most of the beautiful costume jewelry she wore. He never forgot birthdays or holidays.

But Mom might forget because she was so busy. I remember sitting down to Thanksgiving dinner and there'd be a call from overseas, where people don't know about our Thanksgiving Day. Dinner would be cold by the time the call finished. She always, always took the call. At Christmas, Easter, Mother's Day, and so on we could count on there being a call as we sat down to dinner. We were expected to understand, because it was business.

Mom's father was abusive. When she needed shoes, he'd take her to the Army Surplus Store and buy her clodhoppers. She never had anything pretty except for what her Aunt Ruth (Dottie's mother's sister) sent. So naturally, having stylish clothes became one of Dottie's most prized rewards and the symbol of her success. Growing up, my friends admired Dottie and told me they wished their moms looked as beautiful as mine.

We loved shopping. And when she was in the hostesses business, she spent a lot of time in stores selling advertising. When a school dance was coming up, she would bring me three beautiful dresses to choose from. They always fit, and I'd love all of them.

Mom loved the business she was in. It was her hobby as well as her vocation. I think at the end she realized she would not get better, not ever be able to resume working in her old, totally-in-charge way. That's why she slipped away so quickly.

We were all important to her and we were all part of the business. Because of this we learned many of life's lessons. She had a lot of business prowess. She had family. She had countless friends among businesspeople. It all kept her life rich.

When Dottie started the Association of Speakers Bureaus, many of the bureaus were competing against each other and not working together. She physically sat two people down and told them, "You two are going to talk to each other and we are going to have this organization." They both told me they were glad Dottie made them do it. When Dottie started it the name was IGAB. Now it's IASB.

Dr. Norman Vincent Peale helped Mom get her first book published. When I was a little girl, she wrote *Never Underestimate the Sell-*

ing Power of a Woman. There were no books for sales women at that time.

Mom often told me, if you want something in life you must visualize it. She taped artwork she envisioned for the cover of that book to her dressing table's mirror. When she finally got the book published, the cover created by Prentice Hall was almost exactly like the one she had conceptualized several years before. Every day, Mom concentrated on the theory of envisioning, of fleshing out abstract ideas with tangible images.

While Dottie was trying to find a publisher, editors actually told her there were no women in sales to buy the book. This attitude was soon proven to be far off the mark. Not many of the first printings reached the bookstores; instead, entire printings were bought out by Tupperware, Mary Kay, and other companies for the tens of thousands of saleswomen they employed. Later on, when Mom founded Royal Publishing, she bought the rights back and took control of her book.

My life was so different from my friends growing up. Yes, we had the house and the pool and kids were invited over to swim. More importantly, I met people and went to places that many never get to experience in a lifetime.

Mom took me along to a National Speaker's Association Conference in Washington, D.C. We were in a big hotel's lobby when Dad called. He had a envelope addressed to me from The National University. I asked Dad to open it and he told me I'd been accepted. I was crying with joy and a man walked over and asked me what was wrong. I told him I had just been accepted to college. He congratulated me warmly. It turned out that he was Representative, later President, Gerald Ford.

Also inspiring and memorable on that trip was hearing many speakers and learning how they've helped so many people.

Michael MacFarlane:

Dottie married Bob Walters, the only man she had ever dated. He served in WWII in the Pioneer Battalion of the 2nd Marine Corps Division in the South Pacific. They landed on enemy-occupied islands to build bridges and clear the way for the landing craft to invade.

They landed on islands like Guadalcanal, Saipan and Tarawa — usually against a deeply entrenched enemy. On Tarawa, his battalion suffered 70% casualties doing what had to be done so the rest of the division could come ashore. That's how deeply the enemy was dug in.

He was decorated three times for bravery. When they were retreating under heavy fire across a shallow coral reef, he went back four or five times to rescue fellow Marines.

To sum up my grandfather's character, he fought in WWII against the Japanese and could have hated them when he returned. But his pre-war neighbors were Japanese, the Hayacoa's, and they were sent to an internment camp and lost their belongings. One of the first things Grandfather did when he returned from the war was to help them get everything back. He went to court and testified on their behalf.

My mother was in college and living on Coronado Island when I was born. She moved back home with Dottie after my birth. I was brought to the house where Dottie and Bob lived and also had their offices. My earliest memories are of being in that busy house.

My grandmother was always there for me and I used to call Dottie my 'Other Mother.' Dottie used to say, my mother gave birth to me but she was really my mother.

I lived in Dottie's home until my Mother remarried when I was five years old and we moved to Ontario, California. Any time the kids needed support at school with meetings, rides to and from, and attending activities, my grandfather would do that when Dottie was out of town. They came to my school in Ontario for special occasions and my graduation. Any time there was a problem, she'd send my grandfather to take care of it. Like with advertising. She had two thousand continuous accounts and there were always about a dozen with credit problems and grandfather would take care of that.

Dottie never thought she was good at math, but she could certainly multiply success.

When just starting out, Dottie tried to sell an ad to the pharmacist who owned the local Rexall Drugstore franchise, but she could never meet up with him. Four separate businesses informed her "You don't have the man we admire most in your column. He's an outstanding businessman and if he's not using your column, then we don't want it either." Dottie knew she must try again.

The Walters tenacity kicked in. Her Scottish blood, inherited from that undaunted grandfather of hers, was moving her towards success. Dottie went back one more time. She saw that the back of the pharmacy was lit up.

Dottie told this story about what happened then.. "There I saw him — white hair and dressed in the distinguished white jacket. She walked back and said, 'Mr. Ahlman, I don't want to sell you anything, I just want you to give me your thoughts on this column. Would you just be so kind as to look at it? The other merchants in town want your opinion. Please, would you?" He shook his head from left to right. His mouth was an upside down U, saying no.

Dottie would continue, "I was devastated and didn't know if I could make it home pushing the kids all that way. I got as far as the soda fountain where there were three empty stools. I slumped down on one and pulled the kids up close so they wouldn't block the aisle. I just sat there wandering what I was going to do.

"The soda jerk came over.

"I said, 'How much for your smallest Coke?'

"Ten cents." That was all I had, so I laid that out and gave the kids a straw so they could drink. They had to be thirsty breathing all that dust.

Two ladies came in and sat down next to me. The one closest to me said, 'What in the world is wrong with you, girl?'

Dottie would go on, "I said, 'We're going to lose our home. I've done everything I can think of. So many merchants in this town respect Mr. Ahlman and he won't even give me his opinion on my column. Four merchants turned me away today. Those four would have finished the house payment. I don't want to lose our little house.'

"The lady said, 'You wait right here.' First she snatched away the column that I had in my hand. She read every word of it. Then she yelled, 'Rueben, get out here!' The pharmacist was her husband!

"Mr. Ahlman, the pharmacist, had been truly generous to every charity -- so much so that his wife had taken over that part of the business.

"I didn't know enough to ask who was in charge of that part of the business," Dottie said.

"Mrs. Ahlman told her husband, 'You give this girl copy for this week. I'll go back and make a check out for two months of ads.' Dottie said she was stunned. Next, Mrs. Ahlman asked Dottie for the names of the four merchants who had turned her away. As soon as Dottie gave her their names, Mrs. Alhman left to place phone calls to each one. She returned to tell Dottie that the merchants were waiting to see her."

That opportunity changed Dottie's life and it came because she refused to give up.

The Ahlmans became good friends with Dottie and Bob. Dottie believed that special people enter our lives at the right time to give each of us a hand.

The biggest opportunities seem to have a special knack of only showing themselves when things are at their bleakest, when life seems dark and out of options. This is when opportunity becomes visible if your eyes are open enough to see it. Great opportunities are just waiting for moments like that. Dottie's was no different.

Dottie often said, "Einstein was right. Solutions are located at hand. They are very close to you. But you have to go after them. They won't sit there by themselves and do it for you. Take hold because you're the one who has to do it. Reach out and don't be afraid to pursue a dream, because it's waiting for you."

Eventually Mr. Ahlman took the soda fountain out of his drug store. My grandfather bought it with the twelve original stools where Dottie got her first big break. My uncle, Michael Walters, and I helped install it in their home, where it was a reminder of the start of Dottie's career. She relished looking at the fountain and showing it to visitors.

Hollywood didn't discover Dottie at a soda fountain. Instead, she discovered success and her own ability to persist at one. It's hard to believe today, but Dottie had to go in front of a judge to get her own checking account! Only because she was a woman.

Dottie and Bob used to take us on vacations in their motor home. We'd visit Indian reservations all over the Southwest. Dottie used to read to me a lot and she would change a character in the book to my name. If there were animals involved, they would be our animals. She would personalize the story.

When I was going to school, every summer I worked full time with her in her business. As a young kid I would do things like stuffing brochures in envelopes for mass mailings. As an adult, I worked with Dottie for seventeen years.

There were invaluable lessons along the way and her attitude of "You can do it," rubbed off on me along with the determination not to let anything get me down, and that I control my own destiny. Like every other person on this planet, my destiny will be what I make of it.

I love her quote, "There's never a lack of money, just a lack of ideas."

Sometimes she talked about how abusive her father was and how difficult it was when he left. He was very selfish. Dottie told me stories about how he almost killed her mother, Lillian, with a piece of iron. Dottie grabbed the iron and gave him a hard knock with it. Within a few minutes he left and they never saw him again. After that Lillian went to work at the local paper which introduced Dottie to publishing.

Dottie started working at age twelve. She worked in retail sales selling shoes and lingerie. She worked in a midnight bakery in high school and was on the newspaper.

She worked in the advertising business connecting newcomers with local businesses and built it up to hundreds of employees all over California making 5,000 calls a month.

Dottie ran that business — a full time job in itself — but during that time she also wrote her first book, *Never Underestimate the Selling Power of a Woman*. Her timing was perfect, because about the time the book was published, a company called Tupperware was just hitting its stride and moving into the big time. They bought out the first printing of her book. Then Dottie sold large numbers of the book to Mary Kay Cosmetics, Avon, Rubbermaid and Amway.

Dottie spoke at every one of the large rallies those companies staged for all of their saleswomen. She was also active in their local meetings. Then there was the second edition, the third edition — it went all over the world.

When I was in the seventh and eighth grade I used to help her with the hospitality meetings. All of the family assisted with different things over the years. My uncle helped with the printing shop in San Diego County and lived on the property there, which we still own. It's a Spanish-style home with rental property next door, so there are two lots. The office was in the main house. My brother manages the apartments there now.

The Hospitality Hostess Business would send a basket out with a newspaper subscription, discount coupons and gifts. I remember filling our storage area and bedrooms with loads of toilet paper to give away to newcomers.

My grandfather, Bob Walters, operated HH Press. They printed all the material for Hospitality Hostesses, and dust jackets for the anthology books we used to publish. During this time, Dottie was traveling the world. She spoke on the platform with Zig Ziglar, W. Clement Stone, Dr. Kenneth McFarland and all the top speakers. She was the only woman speaker for some time. She became a founding member of the National Speaker's Association, and was also becoming active assisting other speakers to set up their engagements.

In the late 1970's business was changing. It was harder to find people at home because women were entering the workforce en masse. It was harder to find employees as well. Women had been working part-time but now they were getting full time jobs outside the home.

Partly for those reasons, the Hospitality Hostess business was getting more difficult to run, and the print shop was ready to close because new technologies had changed the way things were done. Dottie sold Hospitality Hostess and started the *Sharing Ideas* Newsletter. At that time, it targeted women speakers to encourage them to stick together. Then a lot of male speakers said, "There are valuable insights here, we want to subscribe." So it grew and grew and grew into the wonderful magazine it is today.

In the 1970's there were all these shyster-like speakers, with their 'step up' seminars. They weren't really backing it up well because their fee was whatever they could get. Dottie brought credibility to the speaking industry. She made it professional instead of a bunch of guys in red ties trying to get what they could out of the audience.

When Dottie wrote *Speak and Grow Rich*, she was the first one to define it as a business. She included what she knew about the business which was everything. I remember what the business was like back then. Dottie added class to the profession. Now I'm developing a plan to license people to present the Speak and Grow Rich Program.

Dottie was in such demand that she was being asked for referrals to other speakers for other topics. She started writing contracts and representing other speakers. Speaking bureaus at the time were basically like old theaters using cheap bargaining techniques, with the sole exception of the large bureau that handled celebrities.

She not only was a Founding Member of the National Speakers Association, Founder of the Los Angeles Chapter of NSA, but also in1984 she founded the IGAB (International Group of Agencies and Bureaus).

She designed the CSP Designation with the National Speaker's Association on the Girl Scout Merit Badges. She loved that you could earn the badges. You could earn as much as you wanted.

She spoke in South Africa, Malaysia, Japan, Singapore, Thailand and Australia — all over the world. We always had adventures on the road in getting from Point A to Point B. Once we couldn't get on a plane and had to drive from Toronto to New York. I flew, drove and shipped — whatever was required to get the job done.

Not only would I cultivate the clients who sponsored her seminars, communicate with them and set up her calendar, but then I would send out marketing material from our end to supplement their marketing. I made sure all the products were at the site and booked all the travel. During this time I was doing all the advertising for *Sharing Ideas* and selling speakers to the bureau.

Dottie was a genius and she taught me everything I know but there were times when I reorganized things for her because she was too close and too distracted by all the demands to be able to step back and see the problem herself.

I created the '*Speak and Grow Rich* Master Weekend.' We started with a one-day *Speak and Grow Rich* Program for $299. Selling that to prospective speakers was a challenge. Dottie also had another seminar on creating speaker products. At that time I became aware of the Learning Annex and involved us with it. We started out with three-hour programs.

Instead of a one-day workshop, why not make it two full days, and have the product seminar as a major section? I also developed the five-day symposium. We ended up having four levels of seminars and our lists were building and product sales were increasing since we were constantly out there speaking. We were also cultivating markets outside the NSA. It was a turning point for us and that's basically what we did until Dottie couldn't do it anymore.

In March of 2006 we were on tour together. In the last year she was slowing down. And the last tour was large cities only and on shorter trips. She did the five-day Symposium in June, 2006.

Her mind was sharp but I could see her losing strength. I was taking her to the doctor every couple of weeks saying, "Find something."

Her last speech was in August, 2006 and she just couldn't keep her thoughts up there on the stage. I basically went up and finished the program for her because I had traveled with her to twenty cities twice a year. When we first started doing this my grandfather came with us a couple of times. He would meet us in San Francisco. She was still seeing clients at the house until October, 2006.

It was hard watching such a vital, sharp-witted person going downhill. But right up to the end she was always cheerful, always kind-hearted, always my wonderful grandmother.

John King:

What I remember about my grandmother above anything else was her work ethic. When I spent the night at her house, Dottie would wake up probably at five in the morning and start working. At about seven she would wake my grandfather and me up, and get us ready to go out to breakfast.

She would be at her computer with a cup of coffee, working away. She did that every day. Calls would come in from other countries on the Fourth of July and Thanksgiving Day but also Easter and Christmas from people who didn't know we were celebrating a holiday. She took every single call. We didn't have an answering machine until around

2005. The phone might ring at nine in the evening and she'd still take the call and conduct business for an hour.

A person always answered the phone, either someone in her office or one of the family. I remember learning how to answer the phone properly before I was six years old. But they didn't allow me to answer it until I was eight or nine. I'd say, "Walter's Speaking Services, how can I help you?"

Since I was about five year old I worked in the warehouse and helped out in the office with sticking address labels on magazines.

My grandmother and grandfather were the biggest cheerleaders I ever had. They were extremely supportive when I was attending culinary school. From the moment I enrolled, I was the best chef to my grandmother. I hadn't even started, and she would tell people I was the most gifted chef in the world. There was no doubt in Dottie's mind that I was the best at what I did. They were proud that I was able to find something I loved to do. They'd do anything they could possibly think of to help me along with that.

Since that time I received the L.A. Times Food Section until a month before she passed. Dottie sent that to me for more than ten years.

I'm extremely lucky to have had strong role models of my grandmother and mother who both found successful careers doing what love.

Dottie helped me get my internship in Australia. She contacted A& A hotels in Sydney and arranged for the internship. She set me up with an apartment and a ride from the airport. It was very helpful to see how people in another country do things.

Dottie is the only one who ever fired me — for putting her on hold. That's the last time I ever put my boss on hold. I was seventeen and there was another call coming in. I put Dottie on hold and she told me never to put your boss on hold and she fired me!

I didn't take it too harshly or anything, but it was a life-long lesson. I never worked for my grandmother after that, and it set me up for what I really wanted to do in life.

I took some trips with my mom and grandfather in his RV but Dottie would be working. She would fly to Singapore or Australia and the second she was done with her business, she flew home.

She wanted the phone answered by a person, not a machine, and whenever she could, she would answer it herself.

Mayleta Walters:

Dottie had a passion for fashion. One bedroom in her home was a dedicated dressing room and closet. Wrapped around the entire room were hat racks, shoe racks, and so on. She kept everything she bought because they were all lovely classic things.

That's how Dottie and I connected. It gave her a chance to talk to a woman who enjoyed fashion as much as she did. Dottie was very business oriented and didn't have a lot of time for girlfriends.

When I visited she'd take me though the closet and she could tell me on which occasion she wore what suit and what year it was. She loved purple and invariably she'd accessorize with a plum or purple scarf. There were shoes to match every outfit as well.

She owned big hats and small hats and must have had a hundred hats and each one was cuter than the next. She did have a favorite, a sailor hat that was hung on her picture at her memorial service.

When Michael and I were married she wore a beautiful plaid Scottish skirt. On the skirt she wore a beautiful half moon pin in ambers, oranges and yellows. I admired it, and she gave me the history of the pin. Sometime later when she came to visit she brought me a box with that beautiful pin inside. I was overwhelmed.

She loved her family so much and was a warm and gracious person. I have a hat-pin collection and so did she so we'd discuss her latest filigree hat pin.

It was great fun to connect with her on a feminine basis.

www.ingramcontent.com/pod-product-compliance
Lightning Source LLC
LaVergne TN
LVHW090939080826
845145LV00003B/811

9781601940087